Endeavor

New Readers Press
A Publishing Division of ProLiteracy

The following teachers participated in pilot testing of Endeavor:

Evelyn Surma, Adult Education Teacher
Anaheim Union High School District, Anaheim, CA

Maria Pagnotta, ABE-GED Professor
Seminole Community College, Sanford, FL

Rachel M. Slavkin, Adjunct Faculty
Seminole Community College, Sanford, FL

Lora Zangari, Professional Development Coordinator
Lancaster Lebanon IU13, Lancaster, PA

Endeavor 3
ISBN 978-1-56420-853-8

Printed in the United States of America
9 8 7 6 5 4 3 2

All proceeds from the sale of New Readers Press materials support literacy programs in the United States and worldwide.

Contributing Author: Vista Resources, Inc.
Developmental Editors: Ellen Northcutt, Donna Townsend
Creative Director: Andrea Woodbury
Production Specialist: Maryellen Casey
Art and Design Supervisor: James P. Wallace
Illustrator: Wendy Rasmussen, represented by Wilkinson Studios, Inc.

Contents

Good Sleep for Good Health

Learning Objectives

In this lesson you will:

■ Learn how to get a good night's sleep.

■ Learn to identify cause and effect.

■ Master the key vocabulary used in the article.

■ Write sentences that tell about a time when you did not sleep well.

Key Vocabulary

avoid *(verb)* to keep away from

disrupt *(verb)* to interrupt; break up

environment *(noun)* everything that surrounds and influences people

exhausted *(adjective)* very tired; worn out

function *(verb)* to operate

quality *(noun)* the degree to which something is good or bad

schedule *(noun)* times when certain events happen

stress *(noun)* worry caused by a difficult situation

substitute *(noun)* a thing that takes the place of another

temporary *(adjective)* lasting a short time; not permanent

Before You Read

You can use active reading strategies to help you understand what you read. When you start reading, ask yourself why you are reading. As you read, think about what you already know about the topic.

Use what you know.

1. Sometimes I have trouble falling asleep because _____

_____

_____

_____

Sometimes I lie in bed and think about everything I need to do. Then I can't fall asleep.

2. One thing that helps me fall asleep is _____

_____

_____

_____

_____

Set a purpose for reading.

1. The title of the article tells me that it will be about _____

_____

_____

_____

_____

_____

My brother drinks coffee all day. I wonder if that's why he has trouble sleeping.

2. This article interests me because _____

_____

_____

_____

_____

_____

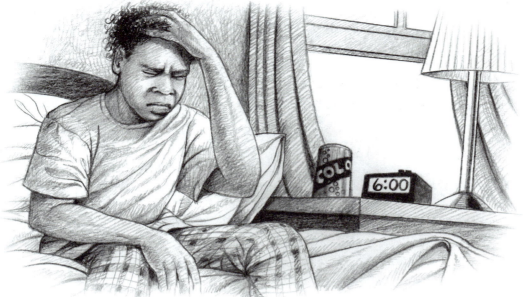

Getting a Good Night's Sleep

Read the article to learn how to get a good night's sleep. Highlight the sentences that tell what happens when people don't sleep well.

Has this ever happened to you? You are lying in bed. You are very tired. But you can't fall asleep. You don't know why. You toss and turn. You think about all kinds of things. Hours go by. Finally you fall asleep. But you end up sleeping for only a few hours. When you wake up, you don't feel rested.

5   Or has this ever happened? You fall asleep right away. Then in the middle of the night you wake up. Suddenly you are wide-awake. You can't go back to sleep. What is happening? You probably have insomnia .

Everyone knows that sleep is important. Without sleep, you don't **function** well. You feel **exhausted.** You have trouble thinking clearly. You have trouble
10 staying focused. You probably feel cranky, too.

Most people need about seven or eight hours of sleep a night. But many people have a hard time getting enough sleep. Some people have trouble falling asleep. Some people wake up in the middle of the night. For some people, the **quality** of their sleep is never good. They still feel tired even if
15 they've slept the whole night.

Sleep problems can happen to anyone. They can be **temporary.** They might last a few weeks or they might last for months. There are many reasons people can't sleep. Sometimes the cause is physical . If someone is in pain, he or she won't be able to sleep.

20 Sometimes it has to do with **stress.** People are often kept up thinking about problems in their lives. And sometimes it might be because of a bad sleep **environment.** If there is too much noise, for example, you might not be able to

insomnia *(noun)*
inability to sleep or remain asleep

physical *(adjective)*
related to the body

sleep. But these are just some possibilities. Sometimes people don't know why they can't sleep.

1. One reason that people have trouble sleeping is _____

   _____

   _____

   _____

   _____

   _____

Continue reading the story. Highlight the sentences that tell what you can do to sleep better.

25   What can you do to get a good night's sleep? Here are some things you can try. Try to go to bed at the same time each night. And get up at the same time each morning. This might seem hard to do. On days off we all want to sleep late. But that can throw off your sleep **schedule.**

   Let's look at an example. Tony stays up until 2:00 A.M. on Saturday night.
30   Then he sleeps until noon on Sunday. What happens then? He has a hard time falling asleep at 11:00 P.M. on Sunday night. He tosses and turns. He finally falls asleep at 1:00 A.M. Then he has to get up at 6:00 A.M. on Monday morning. He's slept for only five hours. That is not a good night's sleep.

   Like Tony, you might not want to go to bed early on the weekends. Then
35   just try to go to sleep at the same time on the weeknights. It could really help you.

   There are other things you can do to get a good night's sleep. Try not to nap during the day. Some people swear by a good "power nap." But this can be bad if you're not getting enough sleep at night. A nap is no **substitute** for a
40   good night's sleep.

2. If you have a good sleep schedule, you _____

   _____

   _____

   _____

   _____

   _____

Finish reading the article to learn more ways to get a good night's sleep.

When you go to bed, give yourself about 20 minutes to fall asleep. If you can't sleep, get up and do something to relax. You might take a bath or drink a glass of warm milk. Go back to bed when you feel sleepy again. The worst thing to do when you can't sleep is to worry that you're not sleeping. Try to
45 think of something that will calm you. You could think about being at the beach or walking in the woods. Or you could try counting sheep. For some people, it really works.

You should **avoid** certain food before bed. Caffeine is known to keep people awake. Caffeine is found in coffee, tea, and many sodas. Even chocolate
50 has caffeine in it. Some people are very sensitive to caffeine. It can keep them awake for hours.

Alcohol can also **disrupt** your sleep. You should not drink alcohol too close to bedtime. It can make you feel sleepy at first. But it makes your sleep much lighter. It can cause you to wake up a lot. A heavy meal can have the
55 same effect.

Too much light can also be a problem. You can use dark shades on your bedroom windows. Some people sleep with eye masks to block out light. Noise can also disrupt your sleep. You can keep a fan on. The hum of the fan will block out noise.
60 Getting a good night's sleep is important. Try to get as much as your body needs. Your health depends on it.

caffeine *(noun)*
a substance in coffee, tea, chocolate, and other drinks that gives people energy

sensitive *(adjective)*
showing a strong reaction to

alcohol *(noun)*
drinks such as beer and wine that can cause changes in people's behavior

3. Some things that keep people awake are _____

_____

_____

_____

_____

4. Which of the suggestions in the article do you think might help you get a better night's sleep?

_____

_____

_____

_____

_____

After You Read

Build a robust vocabulary.

Matching Words   Match the words with their definitions. Write the letter.

_____ 1. schedule

a. everything that surrounds and influences people

_____ 2. quality

b. times when certain events happen

_____ 3. environment

c. the degree to which something is good or bad

_____ 4. function

d. to operate

_____ 5. disrupt

e. to interrupt an activity

Sentence Completions   Complete each sentence using a word from the box.

avoid	disrupt	environment	exhausted	function
quality	schedule	stress	substitute	temporary

1. Tony worked so hard that he was _____ by the end of the day.

2. Skim milk is a good _____ for whole milk.

3. I hope the noise outside is only _____ and won't last too long.

4. Losing your job can cause you a lot of _____.

5. The doctor told Stella she should _____ drinks with caffeine in them.

Word Building   Look at the words in the box. What is the same about them?

books	matches	gloves	boxes

All of the words in the box are **plurals.** A plural names more than one person, place, or thing. Often you add -*s* to the end of a word to make it plural. Sometimes you add -*es*.

Circle the plural ending in each of the words in the box above.

Write the plural of each word below. The first one is done for you.

1. dish: _dishes_____

2. apple: _____

3. desk: _____

4. bunch: _____

5. boss: _____

TIP: Not every word that ends in -s is plural. For example, the word *glass* ends in -s, but is not a plural. *Glasses* is the plural form of *glass*. Read nearby words to see if the word refers to more than one thing.

Writing Activity   Complete this paragraph by using words from the word list on page 5. Reread the definitions, if necessary.

Sometimes I can't fall asleep because of _____. Certain foods and

drinks can also _____ my sleep. When I don't get enough sleep I feel

_____ the next day. Then it is hard for me to _____

well at work. I should _____ drinking caffeine before bedtime.

Think about your reading.

Check your comprehension.   Answer each question. If you don't know the answer, reread the lines in parentheses.

1. How many hours of sleep do most people need? **(line 11)**

   _____

2. How long can sleep problems last? **(lines 16–17)**

   _____

3. How does alcohol affect your sleep? **(lines 52–54)**

   _____

4. How can keeping a fan on in your room help you sleep? **(lines 58–59)**

   _____

Use reading skills: Identify cause and effect.

The **cause** is why something happens. The **effect** is what happens as a result of the cause. In this article, the writer explains the causes of insomnia and many of its effects.

Identify cause and effect. Read the paragraph. Look for both causes and effects:

> There are many reasons people can't sleep. Sometimes the cause is physical. If someone is in pain, he or she won't be able to sleep. Sometimes it has to do with stress. People are often kept up thinking about problems in their lives.

1. Identify a cause in the paragraph.

_____

2. Identify an effect in the paragraph.

_____

Use a graphic organizer.

Fill in the missing information in the chart below.

Cause	Effect
1. Amy drinks two cups of coffee right before bed.	She can't fall asleep for hours.
2. She wears an eye mask when she goes to sleep.	
3. People outside her bedroom window often play loud music.	
4. She wakes up at noon on Sunday afternoon.	

Write About It

Write sentences.

Think about a time when you had trouble falling asleep. Write five sentences that describe your experience.

Prewriting   On you own or with a partner, write some causes and effects that will help you write your sentences. Fill in the graphic organizer with your ideas. Think of what causes sleep problems. List the effect of each cause.

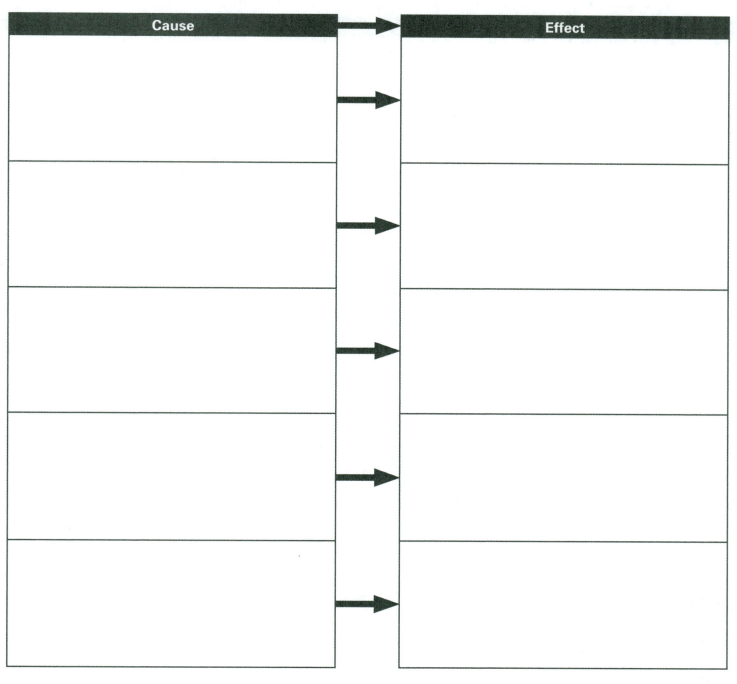

Cause	Effect

Thinking Beyond Reading Think about these questions and discuss them with a partner. Add ideas to the graphic organizer as you talk.

- What caused you to stay awake?

- How did it make you feel?

- What did you do to try to fall asleep?

- What finally worked?

Write your sentences.   Write your final sentences. Use the details in your chart to help you write. Remember that a sentence expresses a complete thought or idea. It always begins with a capital letter. It always ends with a punctuation mark. Usually it ends with a period or a question mark. Sometimes it ends with an exclamation point.

_____

_____

_____

_____

_____

_____

_____

_____

_____

_____

_____

_____

_____

_____

Revise and edit.   Check your sentences for these points:

- Did you write in complete sentences?

- Do your sentences relate to each other?

- Did you use correct spelling and punctuation in your sentences?

A New Way to Work

Learning Objectives

In this lesson you will:

■ Learn how assembly lines changed the way work is done.

■ Learn to classify information.

■ Master the key vocabulary used in the article.

■ Write sentences about working on Henry Ford's assembly lines.

Key Vocabulary

afford *(verb)* to be able to pay for

computers *(noun)* electronic machines that store, sort, and work with information at a high speed

expensive *(adjective)* costing a lot of money

factories *(noun)* buildings where products are made by machines

mechanics *(noun)* people whose job is to make and repair tools, machines, and motors

robots *(noun)* mechanical devices that perform tasks

salary *(noun)* a fixed amount of money paid at regular times for the work a person does

skilled *(adjective)* having the ability to do something well, especially because of training or practice

technology *(noun)* products that are developed using knowledge from science and industry

unskilled *(adjective)* not needing a special skill or training

Before You Read

Look at the title of the article and the picture. Ask yourself an active reading question, "What does this article seem to be about and what do I already know about the topic?"

Use what you know.

1. I know that cars are made in _____

   _____

   _____

   _____

   _____

I know that cars are made in factories. There must be a lot of people working on them.

2. It takes a lot of workers to make cars because _____

   _____

   _____

   _____

   _____

Ask yourself questions.

1. What did Henry Ford do that was different?

   _____

   _____

   _____

   _____

   _____

My cousin Becky worked in a factory. The factory didn't make cars, but all factories are probably a lot alike.

2. What is an assembly line?

   _____

   _____

   _____

   _____

   _____

Moving Things Along

Read the following article about Henry Ford's car factory. Underline details in the article that you already know that help you connect to the topic.

Did you ever wonder how cars are made? Where do all the parts come from? Who puts them together? Today, thousands of cars are made each day. There are many different car companies. People work in **factories** to make cars. It is not hard to make lots of cars in one day. But years ago, it took a very
5 long time.

Most work was different long ago. People worked on things from start to finish. Think of a clay pot as an example. It would take one person to make a clay pot. First the potter would mold the clay. Then he would heat it. Then he would paint it. It could take more than a day to make one pot. It would
10 take a very long time to make hundreds of pots. It was the same with many other products.

In 1893, two brothers built the first car in the United States. Yet even ten years later, there were very few cars on the road. They were **expensive** to make, so they were expensive to buy. Only very rich people could **afford** cars. Others
15 could not.

Henry Ford started a car company in 1903. It was in Detroit. His company made only a few cars a day. Two or three men worked on each car. They worked on it from start to finish. These cars were expensive. But Henry Ford wanted to make a new kind of car. It would be one that anyone could afford.
20 He said, "I will build a motor car for the great multitude."

multitude *(noun)*
the common people

1. The reason that the first cars were very expensive was because _____

_____

_____

_____

_____

assembly line *(noun)*
a way of putting together a product in a factory

conveyor belt *(noun)*
a machine with a continuous moving part that carries things from one place to another

Continue reading the article to find out how Henry Ford changed the way cars were made. Keep underlining details in the article that you already know.

The old way of making cars only produced a few cars a day. So in 1913 Henry Ford came up with a new system. It was called an assembly line . Workers stood in place. A car body was placed on a conveyor belt . The car moved past each worker. The worker added one part to the car. The next
25 worker added another part. By the end of the line, the car would be complete.

Cars moved down the line all day. Workers continued to put the same part on each car. The conveyor belt was carefully timed. This kept the line moving smoothly. No one had to wait. They could keep working as each car moved along.

30 Now each worker only needed to do one job. It might be putting on the tires. Or it might be putting in the seats. Each person became good at his job. That is because he did it a lot. He could do that job much faster. This meant that cars were made faster. Ford's factory could make more cars each day. Soon, it took just three minutes to make a new car!

35 The assembly line changed the way cars were made. It also caused the price of cars to go down. In 1927, Ford's Model T car cost just $290. This was a good price. Almost any family could afford it. Suddenly it was possible for anyone to own a car.

This new way of working also helped to cut costs in the factory. Ford was
40 able to offer his workers a good **salary.** They were paid better than at most other factories. Other car companies wanted to do well. They started using the assembly line, too. Soon all car companies had changed. They all made cars the way Ford did. It took lots of people to create a car, so there were many new jobs. Those workers were also paid well.

2. Working at Ford's factory was a good job because _____

_____

_____

_____

_____

Finish reading the article to find out how Ford's assembly line spread to other factories.

45   Ford's idea was used later in other kinds of factories. This helped lower the prices of other things, too. It also created more jobs for people.

      Ford's assembly line changed factories forever. It changed factory workers, too. Before assembly lines, most factory workers were **skilled.** They were carpenters. Or they were **mechanics.** They needed special training to do their

50   jobs. Now people who worked in factories could be **unskilled.** They needed to learn only one job. They could be very good at this job. But they did not need to learn any other jobs.

      Today many factories use assembly lines. But there have been other changes, too. Sometimes a few workers work together. They work on one

55   thing. But they all do a few jobs. This helps keep the work more interesting. **Technology** has also changed assembly lines. **Robots** can do some jobs now. **Computers** help run some of the machines. Products can be made even faster. New factories run fast. They are faster than even Henry Ford could have imagined.

3. Ford changed the way factory work was done by _____

_____

_____

_____

_____

_____

_____

4. How do you think technology will continue to improve factory work?

_____

_____

_____

_____

_____

_____

After You Read

Build a robust vocabulary.

Matching Words   Match the words with their definitions. Write the letter.

_____ 1. robots

a. a fixed amount of money paid at regular times for the work a person does

_____ 2. factory

b. products that are developed using knowledge from science and industry

_____ 3. unskilled

c. a building where products are made by machines

_____ 4. technology

d. not needing a special skill or training

_____ 5. salary

e. mechanical devices that perform tasks

Sentence Completions   Complete each sentence using a word from the box.

afford	computers	expensive	factory	mechanic
robot	salary	skilled	technology	unskilled

1. A carpenter is an example of a _____ worker.

2. I don't think we can _____ a new car.

3. These $70 shoes are very _____.

4. I need a _____ to work on my car.

5. We use _____ at work to look up information.

Word Building   Look at the following words. What is the same about all of them?

friend	friendly	unfriendly	friendship

Each word has the same **root,** or base word. The root can help you figure out a word's meaning. Underline the root in each word above. Compare answers with a partner. Discuss what each word means. Use the meaning of the root word to help you define the word.

Read these words. Draw a circle around the root word in each word. Use the meaning of the root word to help you understand its meaning.

view	preview	views	viewing

Complete each of the sentences by choosing a word from the box above.

1. I will be _____ that movie tomorrow.

2. We saw a _____ of the new movie.

TIP: When you read, you may find a long word that you do not know. Does the word have a root that you do know? Look closely to see if the root word hints at the word's meaning.

Writing Activity   Complete this paragraph by using words from the word list on page 15. Reread the definitions, if necessary.

The first cars made were very _____. Henry Ford changed

the way _____ made cars. He wanted people to be able to

_____ his cars. He used _____ workers to build the cars.

Today new _____ allows cars to be made even faster.

Think about your reading.

Check your comprehension.   Answer each question. If you don't know the answer, reread the lines in parentheses.

1. When did Henry Ford start his car company? (line 16)

   _____

2. What new idea did Henry Ford come up with for his factory? (lines 21–25)

   _____

3. How long did it take to make a car in Henry Ford's improved factory? (line 34)

   _____

4. What do factories use computers for today? (line 57)

   _____

Use reading skills: Classify information.

When you **classify** information, you organize the information in different ways. You can classify jobs as night jobs or day jobs, for example. You can classify jobs as office work or factory work.

Classify information.   Read the following paragraph. Then complete the sentences.

Before assembly lines, most factory workers were skilled. They were carpenters. Or they were mechanics. They needed special training to do their jobs. After assembly lines, workers in factories could be unskilled. They needed to learn one job. They could be very good at this job. But they did not need to learn any other jobs.

1. Carpenters and mechanics are similar because they are both _____

    _____

2. Factory workers are similar because they are _____

    _____

3. All the workers described above are similar because they _____

    _____

Use a graphic organizer.

You can use a chart like the one below to classify information. Fill in the chart by classifying the following workers as skilled or unskilled: plumbers, mechanics, convenience store clerks, laborers, carpenters, plumber's assistants, drivers, stock persons, farm workers, teachers.

Skilled Workers	Unskilled Workers
Plumbers	Convenience store clerks

Write About It

Write sentences.

Think about what it would have been like to work on Henry Ford's assembly line. Write five sentences that describe your experience.

Prewriting   On your own or with a partner, write some details that will help you write your sentences.

1. What part of the car would you want to work on?

    _____

2. Would you want to build a whole car or part of a car?

    _____

3. How do you feel about doing the same job every day?

    _____

4. Fill in the graphic organizer with details about working on the assembly line.

Main Idea
Today I worked on an assembly line doing _____

Detail	Detail	Detail
The job I do is _____	What I like	What I don't like

Thinking Beyond Reading   Think about these questions and discuss them with a partner. Add ideas to the graphic organizer as you talk.

- How does it feel to work on an assembly line?

- Does anyone work with you?

- How long does it take to do your job?

Write your sentences.   Write your final sentences. Use the details in your chart to help you write. Remember that a sentence expresses a complete thought or idea. It always begins with a capital letter. It always ends with a punctuation mark. Usually it ends with a period or a question mark. Sometimes it ends with an exclamation point.

_____

_____

_____

_____

_____

_____

_____

_____

_____

_____

_____

_____

_____

_____

Revise and edit.   Check your sentences for these points:

- Did you write in complete sentences?

- Do your sentences relate to each other?

- Did you use correct spelling and punctuation in your sentences?

A Family Visit

Learning Objectives

In this lesson you will:

▨ Read a story about relatives coming to stay with a family.

▨ Learn to make judgments.

▨ Master the key vocabulary used in the story.

▨ Write sentences that tell about a time when relatives stayed with you.

Key Vocabulary

anxious *(adjective)* feeling worried and nervous

behavior *(noun)* the way a person acts

cramped *(adjective)* having little space in which to move

firmly *(adverb)* strongly; not likely to be changed

glanced *(verb)* took a quick look

obvious *(adjective)* easy to see or understand

patient *(adjective)* able to stay calm

recognized *(verb)* knew from an earlier experience

relatives *(noun)* people who belong to the same family

scattered *(verb)* thrown around in different directions

Before You Read

Be an active reader. See if you can predict what will happen in the story. As you read, check your prediction. You can also think about people you know who have had similar experiences.

Use what you know.

THINK ABOUT IT

1. People who move to the United States sometimes stay with relatives

   because _____

   _____

   _____

   _____

   _____

I remember when my friend's cousin moved here. He lived with my friend for a few months until he could find a job and an apartment. I wonder if that happens a lot.

2. Do you know people who stayed with their relatives? Tell what happened.

   _____

   _____

   _____

   _____

   _____

   _____

   _____

Make predictions as you read.

THINK ABOUT IT

1. When I look at the picture on page 27, I think this story will be about

   _____

   _____

   _____

   _____

   _____

   _____

The title of the story makes me think that it is about cousins coming to live with their relatives. I will read to find out if I am right.

The Cousins Come to Stay

Read the story to find out what happens when Jackie's relatives arrive. Highlight or underline the actions that you agree with.

It was Monday morning and Jackie Sanchez had just gotten off the phone. She had a lot to think about. Jackie's two kids had already left for school. Her younger sister Lizette was getting ready for work. It was definitely time to tell Lizette the news.

5   "I have some good news," said Jackie. "Juan and Marisol are coming from Puerto Rico. They're finally moving here."

"It's about time!" said Lizette. "So where are they going to stay?"

Jackie didn't answer for a minute. She looked **anxious.** Then she said, "Here?"

Lizette jumped up. "Jackie, you didn't!" she cried. "Are you crazy? We have
10 no room for them here. What are you going to do?"

"Lizette, what was I supposed to say? They're our cousins!"

"You could have said no. You could have told them to find a hotel or something." Lizette squeezed through the **cramped** room to reach the closet.

Jackie looked angry. "Now, you're the one who's crazy. You think they can
15 afford a hotel? Why do you think they're moving? Look, they won't be here for long."

"How long do you think?" said Lizette.

"Well," said Jackie with a sigh. "I don't know."

1. Jackie is anxious at the beginning of the story because _____

   _____

   _____

Continue reading to find out what Jackie does next. Highlight or underline phrases that show a character who is acting in a way that you agree with.

That night Jackie told her kids the news. They were not pleased.

20 "Are you serious?" moaned Joe, who was sixteen. "Where are they going to sleep?"

"We'll find room," said Jackie. "It's only for a short time, OK?"

"Mom, I'm not sleeping on the couch!" said Lola, her fourteen year old.

"See Jackie, I told you this would be a big deal," said Lizette, stepping in.

25 "You can't just move people in here without anyone reacting."

"All right! All of you, can you just be **patient?** It's not forever. It's temporary. Why should we send our cousins anywhere else? When our mother came here from Puerto Rico, where do you think she lived? You know where, don't you Lizette? With Aunt Lula and Uncle Eduardo. If she hadn't had a

30 place to stay, you and I wouldn't be here right now. You kids wouldn't be here, either. So what do you think of that?"

Everyone looked at Jackie, but no one said anything. They knew that when she had made up her mind, she was not going to change it easily.

The next morning Jackie had a talk with her kids before they left for

35 school. "I know we don't have a lot of space here, but we're going to be fine. I think it could even be fun to have **relatives** staying here. But there's something we need to talk about."

Joe and Lola **glanced** at each other.

"You're going to have to help with whatever needs to get done, OK?"

40 Jackie said **firmly.**

"But, Mom—" began Joe.

"No, wait, don't say anything yet. I'm counting on you to be helpful, all right? Do you think you can do that?" Jackie asked them, her voice growing angry.

45 "I guess," said Joe, as he shrugged .

"OK," said Lola, hesitantly .

"Good!" said Jackie. "They'll be here on Friday and I expect you to be on your best **behavior!**"

2. When Jackie's cousins arrive, I think that Jackie will be _____

_____

_____

Finish reading the story to see if your predictions are correct.

On Friday morning Jackie was frantic . She had to rush to catch the bus

50 to the airport. She ran around the airport trying to find the right gate to meet her cousins.

shrugged (verb)
raised and lowered the shoulders to show uncertainty

hesitantly (adverb)
acting slowly and uncertainly

frantic (adjective)
very fast and not very organized

Finally she saw Juan and Marisol. It had been a long time since she'd seen them. But she **recognized** them from pictures.

The biggest surprise was Marisol. Her belly was huge. It was **obvious** that
55 she was pregnant. Jackie greeted her cousins with a big hug. "We have to find you your own place fast!" said Jackie, looking at Marisol's belly. They all laughed. Then Jackie said, "OK, listen, I'm going to take you back to the apartment. Then I have to go to work. You guys can get settled. I'll be home around 6:00. We have a lot of catching up to do."

60 Juan and Marisol had only a few bags with them. They had left most of their things in Puerto Rico. They brought only the things they needed right away.

When Jackie got home from work, she was greeted by a delicious smell. She glanced at the mess all over the living room. She stepped over the bags
65 and sleeping bags and clothes that were **scattered** all over the floor.

She headed for the tiny kitchen. There she found everyone in the middle of making a meal. Marisol was stirring a pot on the stove. Juan was taking something out of the refrigerator. Lizette was measuring something into a bowl. Even Joe and Lola had been put to work, chopping peppers and onions.

70 "What's going on in here?" Jackie asked, stunned.

"Oh, nothing," said Marisol, with a grin. "We just thought you might like a real Puerto Rican meal tonight."

Lizette turned to Jackie with a huge smile. "You're not going to believe all the stuff we made. It's going to be delicious!"

75 "Come have a taste!" said Juan.

"I'm not sure I'll fit in the kitchen!" Jackie said, laughing. Marisol held a spoon out to Jackie and she took a taste. "Mm," said Jackie. "That is delicious."

Lizette said, "I told them that if they promise to cook like this every night, we can certainly find room for Marisol's baby when he's born."

80 "I can sleep on the couch!" said Lola. Everyone laughed, Jackie the loudest of all.

3. After Jackie saw her sister and her kids cooking with their cousins, she felt

_____

_____

_____

4. Do you think it will be easy or hard for Jackie's family to have their cousins stay with them? Explain.

_____

_____

_____

After You Read

Build a robust vocabulary.

Matching Words   Match the words with their definitions. Write the letter.

_____ 1. behavior

_____ 2. firmly

_____ 3. obvious

_____ 4. anxious

_____ 5. recognized

a.   knew from an earlier experience

b.   easy to see or understand

c.   the way a person acts

d.   feeling worried and nervous

e.   strongly

Sentence Completions   Complete each sentence using a word from the box.

anxious	behavior	cramped	firmly	glanced
obvious	patient	recognized	relatives	scattered

1.   Linda has many _____ on her mother's side.

2.   His _____ apartment doesn't have enough space for that big TV.

3.   Please be _____ and wait until I'm ready.

4.   The papers were _____ all over the desk.

5.   Joe quickly _____ around the room, but he didn't see his friends.

Word Building   A **prefix** is a group of letters added to the beginning of a word. When you add a prefix to a word, you make a new word with a new meaning. For example, the prefix *un-* means "not," *unkind* means "not kind."

Circle the prefix in each word in the box below.

unhealthy	unlikely	unnecessary	unopened	unwilling

Complete each of the sentences below by choosing a word from the box. The first one is done for you.

1. It's _unhealthy_____ to eat a lot of fried food.

2. Paul was _____ to go out late last night.

3. It was _____ for Rita to get a new driver's license because she found her old one.

4. The box of crackers was _____.

5. I think it's _____ to rain tonight.

TIP: When you read, you may notice words with prefixes. If you remember what the prefix means, you can probably guess the meaning of the word.

Writing Activity   Complete this paragraph by using words from the word list on page 25. Reread the definitions, if necessary.

Last year my _____ came to live with my family. I had never met

them before, yet I _____ them from all the pictures they had sent.

My cousin had to share my _____ bedroom with me. At first I was a little

_____ about meeting him. But it soon became _____

that we would get along well.

Think about your reading.

Check your comprehension.   Answer each question. If you don't know the answer, reread the lines in parentheses.

1. Who is coming to live with Jackie and her family? (lines 5–11)

   _____

2. Where are Jackie's relatives moving from? (lines 5–6)

   _____

3. What does Jackie notice about Marisol at the airport? (lines 54–55)

   _____

4. What is everyone doing when Jackie gets home from work? (lines 63–67)

   _____

Use reading skills: Make judgments.

When you read, you may find that you form opinions about what you read. When you do that, you **make judgments.** You might make a judgment about a character. For example, you might decide that a character is good or bad. You might decide if you agree with something a character did.

Make judgments.   Make judgments about the characters in the story.

1. I think that Jackie's decision to have her cousins live with her was _____

_____

2. I think that Lizette's reaction to her cousins coming was _____

_____

3. The character I most agree with is _____

_____

4. I agree with this character because _____

_____

Use a graphic organizer.

Fill in the missing information in the chart below.

What the Story Tells Me	What I Think About the Information
Jackie decides to have her cousins stay with her in her small apartment.	I think that Jackie made the right decision.
Jackie's sister and her kids are not happy that their cousins will be staying with them.	
Jackie's cousins make a big meal for Jackie their first night in her apartment.	

Write About It

Write sentences.

Think about a time when a relative came to visit or stay with you for a while. Write five sentences that describe your experience.

Prewriting On your own or with a partner, write some ideas that will help you write your sentences. Fill in the graphic organizer with your ideas. Try to remember exactly what happened.

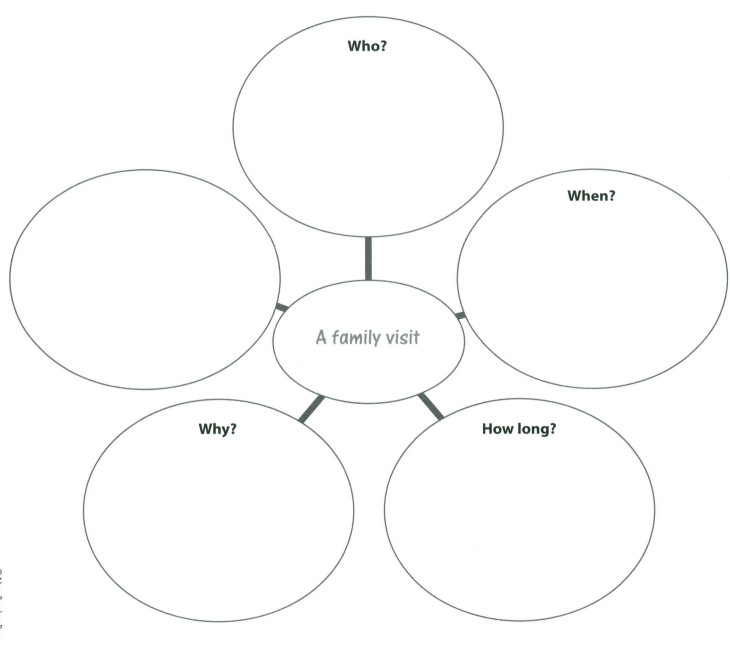

Thinking Beyond Reading   Think about these questions and discuss them with a partner. Add ideas to the graphic organizer as you talk.

- How many people lived together when your relatives visited you?

- How comfortable was everyone?

- How did the extra work get done around the house?

- How did everyone feel about the visit?

Write your sentences.   Write your final sentences. Use the details in your graphic organizer to help you write. Remember that a sentence expresses a complete thought or idea. It always begins with a capital letter. It always ends with a punctuation mark. Usually it ends with a period or a question mark. Sometimes it ends with an exclamation point.

_____

_____

_____

_____

_____

_____

_____

_____

_____

_____

_____

_____

_____

Revise and edit.   Check your sentences for these points:

- Did you write in complete sentences?

- Do your sentences relate to each other?

- Did you use correct spelling and punctuation in your sentences?

Connecting a Community

Learning Objectives

In this lesson you will:

◾ Learn about how a community helped an artist paint a bridge.

◾ Learn to draw conclusions.

◾ Master the key vocabulary used in the article.

◾ Write sentences that tell about an object or a place that represents the spirit of community.

Key Vocabulary

assistants *(noun)* helpers

community *(noun)* a particular area where a group of people live

information *(noun)* knowledge or facts about something

local *(adjective)* having to do with a particular place such as a neighborhood or town

represents *(verb)* is a symbol of something

retired *(adjective)* having given up a job or life of work

stranger *(noun)* a person you do not know

teenage *(adjective)* between the ages of 13 and 19

volunteers *(noun)* people who work or help without pay

web site *(noun)* a resource on the World Wide Web that tells you about a topic

Before You Read

As you read the title and look at the picture, remember to use what you already know about the topic of the article. Ask yourself active reading questions before, during, and after reading the article. You can make notes. You can write down questions in the margins.

Use what you know.

1. I know about a community that _____

   _____

   _____

   _____

   _____

I know that there are all kinds of bridges, but they all usually connect one place to another.

2. A bridge I know about is _____

   _____

   _____

   _____

   _____

Ask yourself questions.

1. The title of the article makes me want to know _____

   _____

   _____

   _____

   _____

I wonder what makes this bridge special.

2. As I read the article, I'd like to find out _____

   _____

   _____

   _____

   _____

The Community Bridge

Read the following article about the Community Bridge in Frederick, Maryland. Jot down any questions you have as you read.

In 1993, artist William Cochran had an idea. He wanted to paint a mural on a bridge. It was just a plain concrete bridge. The bridge was in Frederick, Maryland. Frederick is not far from Washington, D.C.

The bridge crossed a creek. This creek divided the **community.** Whites
5 lived on one side. African Americans lived on the other. Cochran wanted to bring the community together. He thought the bridge might be the answer.

One day, Cochran also thought of a question. He was walking by the bridge. He saw some **teenage** boys there. He told them he wanted some ideas for his project. He said, "What object **represents** the spirit of community to you?"

10 One boy answered. He said, "Two hands—one black and one white. One helping the other over the wall. Doesn't matter which is which."

Cochran had asked this question before. But this was the first time he'd asked a **stranger.** He liked the answer he got. He thought it was just right. He could paint this on the bridge.

15 Then he had an idea. Maybe other people had good answers. He would ask the question to as many people as possible.

William Cochran wanted to ask the question to everyone in Frederick. It would be their bridge. They should decide what it looked like.

He got together a group of **volunteers.** The group came from all over the
20 community. They were high school students. They were **retired** people. They were shop owners. All of them helped with the project.

mural *(noun)*
   a large painting
   on a wall

concrete *(noun)*
   a hard, strong
   building material

They put up posters. They sent out letters. They sent out **information** to all the **local** schools. They asked the question. "What object represents the spirit of community to you?" Then they waited for the answers.

1. Cochran wanted everyone in Frederick to answer his question because

_____

_____

_____

_____

Continue reading the article to find out some answers to Cochran's question. Jot down more questions as you read. Look for answers to your questions.

25 Cochran didn't stop there. He wanted everyone to see the question. People wrote it in colored chalk on sidewalks. For six weeks, the question was on an electric sign. The sign was near a major highway. Everyone could see it.

Soon the story of the bridge was everywhere. It was in magazines. Newspapers wrote about it. Some television shows talked about it. Thousands 30 of answers came in. Cochran's group also started a **web site.** Anyone in the world could send in ideas.

The Community Bridge was finished in 1998. Cochran used close to 1,000 of the ideas sent in. The most popular idea was two clasped hands. Many people felt that this was an important symbol of community.

35 Other people thought of flowers. Some thought of fruits. Some thought of stars. There were many more ideas. All of them were added to the bridge.

clasped *(verb)*
held firmly and tightly

2. People put Cochran's question on signs, posters, and even sidewalks

so that _____

_____

_____

_____

3. Another question I have about the Community Bridge is _____

_____

_____

_____

_____

Finish reading the article to see if your questions will be answered.

Cochran worked on the bridge for five years. He had help from **assistants.**
They used a special technique . The technique fools the eye. They painted flat
pictures, but the pictures look as if they were carved into the bridge.

40   Many people walk by the bridge every day. They never realize they have
been fooled. They think they are looking at an old stone bridge.

The bridge looks like it has thousands of carvings on it. It has ivy leaves
painted on it. The ivy looks real. There are doors on the bridge. There is a
fountain. All these things look real. People have to look up close. Then they

45 see that all the art on the bridge is painted.

Cochran liked that the bridge tricked the eye. He thought this was
important. Many times we are fooled. We look at people. We think they will
act a certain way. Yet this is often not true.

Cochran was surprised to find that so many of the ideas for the bridge

50 were the same. Yet they came from different parts of the community. Cochran
believed that the bridge helped bring the community together.

The bridge helps the community in other ways, too. It brings visitors.
Thousands of people come to Frederick each year. People come because they
have heard about the bridge. They have read about it. Or they have seen

55 pictures of it. They come to Frederick to see it in person.

When people visit the city, they spend money. This helps the city. The
community had helped William Cochran paint the bridge. Now the bridge was
helping the community. It was a true Community Bridge.

technique (noun)
a particular way of
doing something

carvings (noun)
pictures created by
cutting or shaping

4. The Community Bridge helps the community of Frederick by _____

_____

_____

_____

_____

5. Do you think your community would like a similar community bridge?
   Tell why or why not.

_____

_____

_____

_____

_____

After You Read

Build a robust vocabulary.

Matching Words   Match the words with their definitions. Write the letter.

_____ 1. volunteers

_____ 2. retired

_____ 3. represents

_____ 4. stranger

_____ 5. community

a.   a person you do not know

b.   having given up a job or life of work

c.   people who work or help without pay

d.   a particular area where a group of people live

e.   is a symbol of something

Sentence Completions   Complete each sentence using a word from the box.

assistants	community	information	local	represents
retired	stranger	teenage	volunteers	web site

1.   I can look up _____ at the library.

2.   They work as _____ to the manager at the store.

3.   My _____ son will graduate from high school soon.

4.   Our _____ movie theater shows good movies.

5.   I can find out more about cats on this _____ about cats.

Word Building   A **suffix** is a group of letters added to the end of a word. When a suffix is added, a new word with a new meaning is formed. The suffix *-ful* means "full of" or "having." *Fearful* means being full of fear. The suffix *-ly* means "in a way." *Sadly* means in a sad way.

Read these words. Each word ends with a suffix. Circle the suffix in each word below. Use the meaning of the suffix to help you figure out what the word means.

joyful	helpful	slowly	kindly

thankful	helpful	safely	quickly

Complete each sentence below by choosing a word that ends with the suffix *-ful* or *-ly*.

1. Sally was very _____ bringing the groceries upstairs.

2. I read _____ to find the answer to my question.

TIP: When you come across a word you do not know, see if the word has a suffix, or ending, you recognize such as *-ful* in *thankful*. If you know what the suffix means, you may be able to figure out the meaning of the word.

Writing Activity Complete this paragraph by using words from the word list on page 35. Reread the definitions, if necessary.

William Cochran wanted to help the _____ of Frederick by painting

a bridge. He got many _____ to help ask a question. He collected

_____ from many different people. He asked his question in all the

_____ schools. He even started a _____ to get ideas

from around the world. Many thought that clasped hands would _____

their community.

Think about your reading.

Check your comprehension. Answer each question. If you don't know the answer, reread the lines in parentheses.

1. Where did William Cochran want to paint a mural? (lines 1–3)

   _____

2. What question did Cochran ask the people in the community to answer? (line 9)

   _____

3. What was the most popular answer to Cochran's question? (line 33)

   _____

4. How many people visit the Community Bridge each year? (line 53)

   _____

Use reading skills: Draw conclusions.

You **draw conclusions** all the time. If you see a fire engine racing down your street, you might draw the conclusion that there is a fire somewhere nearby. When readers draw a conclusion, they try to figure out something by using clues from the text and using what they know from their own experiences.

Draw conclusions. When you read this section of the article, you can see the conclusion the author draws about the bridge:

> The community had helped William Cochran paint the bridge. Now the bridge was helping the community. It was a true Community Bridge.

1. The community helped by _____

   _____

2. The bridge helped the community by _____

   _____

3. Conclusion: The bridge is a "true Community Bridge" because _____

   _____

Use a graphic organizer.

Fill in the missing information in the chart below.

Clue	William Cochran wanted everyone in the community to give ideas for the bridge.
What I Already Know	There can be problems in a community if people don't get along.
Conclusion	1.

Clue	The bridge's mural tricks the eye.
What I Already Know	Many people don't look closely at things as they pass by.
Conclusion	2.

Write About It

Write sentences.

Think about William Cochran's question in the article. What object represents the spirit of community to you? Write five sentences. The first sentence will answer the question and the other sentences will explain your answer.

Prewriting   On your own or with a partner, write the details that you will include in your description. Fill in the graphic organizer with your ideas.

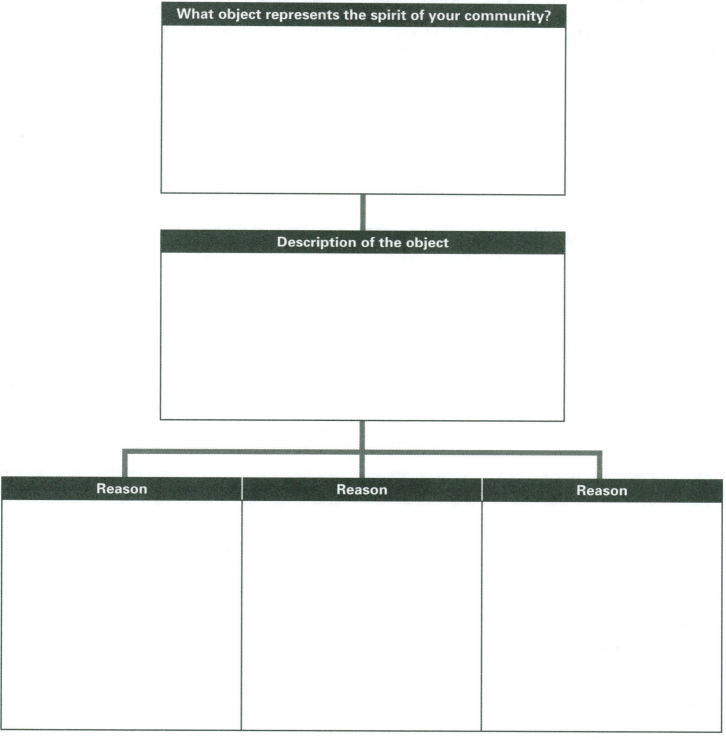

What object represents the spirit of your community?

Description of the object

Reason	Reason	Reason

Thinking Beyond Reading Think about these questions and discuss them with a partner. Add ideas to the graphic organizer as you talk.

- What object did you choose?

- Why did you choose that object?

- What does the object mean to you?

- Do you think others in your community would agree with your choice? Why or why not?

Write your sentences. Write your final sentences. Use the ideas in your chart to help you write. Remember that a sentence expresses a complete thought or idea. It always begins with a capital letter. It always ends with a punctuation mark. Usually it ends with a period or a question mark. Sometimes it ends with an exclamation point.

_____

_____

_____

_____

_____

_____

_____

_____

_____

_____

_____

_____

_____

Revise and edit. Check your sentences for these points:

- Did you write in complete sentences?

- Do your sentences relate to each other?

- Did you use correct spelling and punctuation in your sentences?

Sing for Your School

Learning Objectives

In this lesson you will:

■ Learn about how a group of singers raised money for their school.

■ Learn to identify main idea and details.

■ Master the key vocabulary used in the article.

■ Write sentences that tell what it might have been like to see the Fisk Jubilee Singers sing.

Key Vocabulary

accept *(verb)* to let join a group, organization, or university

audience *(noun)* a group of people gathered to hear or see something

concert *(noun)* a performance of music in front of an audience

earned *(verb)* received money for work completed

education *(noun)* the knowledge a person gets through learning

generation *(noun)* all the people who were born around the same time

permanent *(adjective)* lasting forever or for a long time

slaves *(noun)* people who are owned by other people

thrilling *(adjective)* very exciting

traditional *(adjective)* according to the beliefs and ways of doing things that have existed for a long time

Before You Read

As an active reader, you can choose from various strategies to help you understand what you're reading. Choose the strategies that work best for you. You may, for example, want to think about why you are reading. Or you may want to think about what you already know about the subject.

Use what you know.

THINK ABOUT IT

1. Years ago, most black Americans were not allowed to go to school

   because _____

   _____

   _____

   _____

I know that many years ago, most black Americans were slaves. They were not allowed to go to school. I think these important facts are background for this article.

2. Freed slaves wanted to go to school so they could _____

   _____

   _____

   _____

   _____

Set a purpose for reading.

THINK ABOUT IT

1. I think this article will explain _____

   _____

   _____

   _____

I've never heard of the Fisk Jubilee Singers. I'd like to know who they are and what they did.

2. I would like to learn about _____

   _____

   _____

   _____

The Fisk Jubilee Singers

Read the article about the Fisk Jubilee Singers. As you read, highlight or underline the most important ideas.

Today just about everyone can go to school. But years ago, most black Americans weren't allowed to get an **education.** That was because they were **slaves.** Most slaves never learned to read or write. But in 1865 the slaves were freed. That meant that they could go to school.

5 Going to school was important to the freed slaves, but it wasn't always easy. Sometimes there were no schools that would **accept** black students. Sometimes there were not enough teachers. Sometimes there just wasn't enough money. That was the problem at Fisk University.

Fisk University was started in 1866, in Nashville, Tennessee. It was the first
10 American university to accept all men and women. When Fisk opened, classes were held in old army hospital buildings. The buildings weren't much. But going to school was a **thrilling** experience for these students.

Five years later, in 1870, money became a serious problem for Fisk. The university needed money to repair old buildings and to build **permanent**
15 buildings. Money could save the school. But where would the money come from?

1. So far, the article has been about _____

_____

_____

_____

Continue reading to find out what the students at Fisk did to earn money for the school. Keep underlining or highlighting the most important ideas.

George White was a music teacher at Fisk University. He decided to create a singing group. He thought the group could travel across the country and sing. Each **concert** they gave would help raise the money that the school needed.

20　The group White started in 1871 was made up of nine Fisk students. He named the group the "Fisk Jubilee Singers." He got the idea for the name from the Bible. The Bible says that in the "year of jubilee," all slaves will be set free. Most of the Fisk students had been slaves. The "Fisk Jubilee Singers" seemed like the perfect name.

25　The Fisk Jubilee Singers began singing all over the country. Their first concerts were held in small towns in the northern states. The group sang popular ballads and **traditional** American songs. The concerts were good, but not very successful.

But George White had an idea. He thought that the group should sing 30　slave songs, the songs of their ancestors . Some of those songs had been sung by slaves for many years. They had been passed down from **generation** to generation.

The Jubilee Singers weren't sure that they wanted to share those songs. But they gave it a try. They began to sing the slave songs called " spirituals ." They 35　sang for people who had never heard spirituals before.

At first people were surprised by the spirituals. But very quickly, they grew to love the songs and the group who sang them. Soon the group started singing in big cities, not just in small towns. In 1872 the President of the United States invited them to sing at the White House.

40　The Jubilee Singers had done something special. They were the first group to sing traditional slave songs in front of an **audience.** As they became famous, they made spirituals popular. This allowed them to keep alive the songs of their past.

ballads (noun)
　　songs that tell a story

ancestors (noun)
　　the people in your family who lived long before you were born

spirituals (noun)
　　religious songs developed by black communities

2. George White was _____

_____

_____

_____

3. The Fisk Jubilee Singers were special because _____

_____

_____

_____

Finish reading the article to find out what how the Fisk Jubilee Singers saved their school.

45
In 1873 White added two more people to the Jubilee Singers. Also in that year, the singers went to Europe for the first time. They performed in Europe for many years. While they were there, they sang for many important and famous people. They even sang for the Queen of England. She thought the music was so beautiful that she cried.

50
The Jubilee Singers **earned** over $50,000 their first year in Europe. It was enough money to save Fisk. The university used that money to build their first permanent building. The building was finished in 1876. It was called Jubilee Hall. It was named after the singers.

Fisk University continues to grow today. And the Jubilee Singers continue to sing new songs as well as the spirituals sung by the first singers.

55
Every October 6, Fisk celebrates Jubilee Day. This is to honor the original Jubilee Singers. Without their help, the school might not be here today.

4. The Fisk Jubilee Singers were able to save their school by _____

_____

_____

_____

_____

_____

5. What do you think would have happened if the Fisk Jubilee Singers hadn't started singing spirituals?

_____

_____

_____

_____

_____

_____

After You Read

Build a robust vocabulary.

Matching Words   Match the words with their definitions. Write the letter.

_____ 1. permanent

_____ 2. slaves

_____ 3. generation

_____ 4. audience

_____ 5. education

a.   all the people who were born around the same time

b.   people who are owned by other people

c.   the knowledge a person gets through learning

d.   a group of people gathered to hear or see something

e.   lasting for a long time

Sentence Completions   Complete each sentence using a word from the box.

accept	audience	concert	earned	education
generation	permanent	slaves	thrilling	traditional

1.   Andrea hopes that the state university will _____ her.

2.   We put the money we _____ this week in the bank.

3.   The roller coaster ride was _____.

4.   My grandmother likes to cook _____ Mexican food.

5.   Marco went to a _____ to hear his favorite band.

Word Building   There are many ways to describe people and things. You can talk about a *tall building* or a *short building*. If you want to compare two things, you usually add *-er* to the word that describes, for example, the *taller building* or the *shorter building*. With words that end in *y*, you change the *y* to *i* when you add *-er*. For example, *easy* becomes *easier*.

Read the words in the box. Circle the ending that shows that the word is comparing two things.

lighter	earlier	richer	heavier

Add an ending to each word below so that it is a word that compares. The first one is done for you.

1. funny: _funnier_

2. quick: _____

3. sharp: _____

4. happy: _____

5. old: _____

TIP: Some describing words cannot be changed by adding -er. If you want to compare two beautiful dresses, you say one is _more beautiful_ than the other. Or you say that one book is _less interesting_ than another.

Writing Activity   Complete this paragraph by using words from the word list on page 45. Reread the definitions, if necessary.

My grandmother went to a _____ of the Fisk Jubilee

Singers. She was one of many people in the _____. The singers

sang _____ songs. They learned the songs from an older

_____. My grandmother said that it was _____ to

be there.

Think about your reading.

Check your comprehension.   Answer each question. If you don't know the answer, reread the lines in parentheses.

1. Why was Fisk University different from other schools? (lines 9–10)

_____

2. What did George White decide to name Fisk's singing group? (line 21)

_____

3. How much money did the Jubilee Singers earn their first year in Europe? (line 49)

_____

4. What was the name of the first permanent building at Fisk University? (lines 50–52)

_____

Use reading skills: Identify main idea and details.

The **main idea** of an article or story tells what it is mostly about. This article is mostly about the Fisk Jubilee Singers. Supporting **details** explain, describe, or give more information about the main idea.

Identify main idea and details. Read the following paragraph from the article about the Jubilee Singers.

> In 1873 White added two more people to the Jubilee Singers. Also in that year, the singers went to Europe for the first time. They performed in Europe for many years. While they were there, they sang for many important and famous people. They even sang for the Queen of England. She thought the music was so beautiful that she cried.

1. Find the sentence that tells the main idea of the paragraph. Underline it.

2. Find a detail in the paragraph above that supports the main idea. Circle it.

3. The author included information about the Jubilee Singers singing for the Queen of England in order to

_____

_____

_____

_____

Use a graphic organizer.

A main idea from the article is written in the diagram below. Fill in the missing details that support the main idea.

Main Idea
The Fisk Jubilee Singers traveled around the country giving concerts.

Supporting Detail	Supporting Detail	Supporting Detail
1. They sang traditional songs.	2.	3.

Write About It

Write sentences.

Imagine what it was like to attend a concert of the Fisk Jubilee Singers in 1872. Suppose they came to your city or town to perform. You knew about the slaves but not their music. Write five sentences that describe what the experience might have been like.

Prewriting   On your own or with a partner, write the details that you will include in your description. Use details from the article to support the main idea. Fill in the graphic organizer with your ideas. At least one detail should describe your feelings and opinion about the concert.

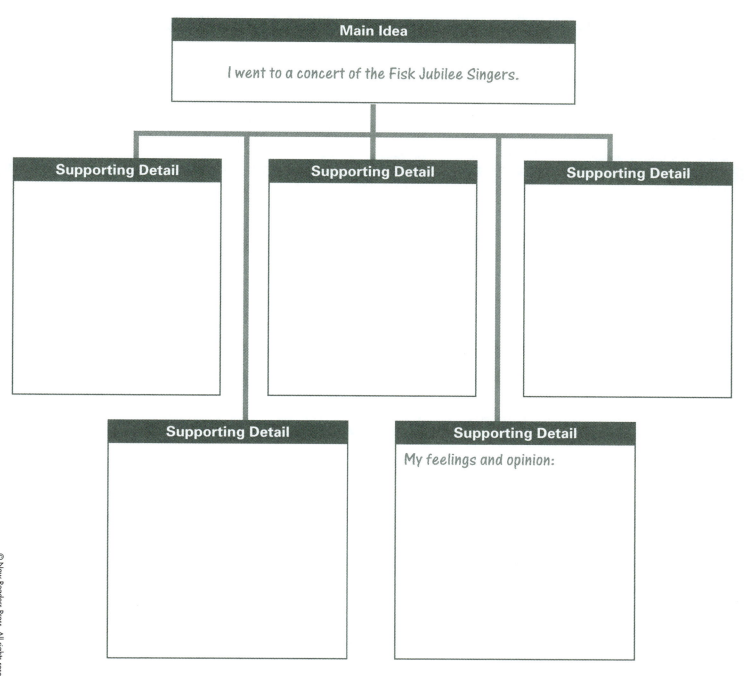

Main Idea

I went to a concert of the Fisk Jubilee Singers.

Supporting Detail

Supporting Detail

Supporting Detail

Supporting Detail

Supporting Detail

My feelings and opinion:

Thinking Beyond Reading   Think about these questions and discuss them with a partner. Add ideas to the graphic organizer as you talk.

- What kind of songs did the Jubilee Singers sing?

- How did the audience show that they liked the music?

- If you had been in the audience for a concert, would you like the music?

- How would the music have made you feel?

Write your sentences.   Write your final sentences. Use the ideas in your diagram to help you write. Remember that a sentence expresses a complete thought or idea. It always begins with a capital letter. It always ends with a punctuation mark. Usually it ends with a period or a question mark. Sometimes it ends with an exclamation point.

_____

_____

_____

_____

_____

_____

_____

_____

_____

_____

_____

_____

_____

Revise and edit.   Check your sentences for these points:

- Did you write in complete sentences?

- Do your sentences relate to each other?

- Did you use correct spelling and punctuation in your sentences?

The Rights of Citizens

Learning Objectives

In this lesson you will:

■ Learn about how to become an American citizen.

■ Learn to compare and contrast.

■ Master the key vocabulary used in the article.

■ Write sentences that tell what it might be like for an adult to become an American citizen.

Key Vocabulary

application *(noun)* a request in writing

apply *(verb)* to make a formal request

approved *(verb)* allowed or OKed

background *(noun)* a person's experience, education, and family history

ceremony *(noun)* a set of actions that someone performs to mark a special occasion

fingerprints *(noun)* prints made by the pattern of ridges on the fingertips

identification *(noun)* something that proves who a person is

permission *(noun)* approval to do something, given by a person with authority

photograph *(noun)* a picture made by a camera

process *(noun)* steps taken to make or do something

Before You Read

Ask yourself, "What do I already know about the topic of this article?" Then ask yourself questions during and after reading, too. Write questions in the margins. You can also write whether you agree or disagree with what you are reading.

Use what you know.

1. Some people want to become American citizens because _____

   _____

   _____

   _____

My aunt Dolores moved here from the Dominican Republic. She became an American citizen last year. I wonder if the process she went through is the same for other people.

2. American citizens are people who _____

   _____

   _____

   _____

   _____

Ask yourself questions.

1. The title of the article makes me want to ask about _____

   _____

   _____

   _____

   _____

This article should have good information. I'm going to look for the things someone has to do to become a citizen.

2. The first paragraph makes me think about _____

   _____

   _____

   _____

   _____

Becoming an American Citizen

Read the following article about becoming an American citizen. Jot down questions that you have as you read.

Were you born in the United States? If you were, then you are an American citizen . That is one way to become a citizen here. But it is not the only way. Some people are born here. Then they move to another country. They live in the other country most of their lives. Yet they are still American
5 citizens. Some people were not born here. Yet their parents were American citizens. This can make them citizens, too.

Some people move here from other countries. They get **permission** to live and work here. Over time, they can become American citizens, too. Yet it can be a long **process.**

10 First, people from other countries decide they want to move here. They **apply** to the American government. They need to be **approved.** Then they get permanent resident cards. These are also called "green cards."

These cards used to be printed on green paper. People started calling them green cards. Now they can be any color. But they are still known as
15 green cards.

A green card is a kind of **identification.** It says that you can live here. It says you can work here. You need to keep the card with you all the time. The card includes your name. It includes your **photograph.** It includes other important information.

20 You can live here for many years with a green card. You can even live here your whole life with one. But you won't have all the rights of citizens. For example, you can't vote. So some people with green cards choose to become citizens.

citizen (noun)
> a person who is a member of a country because of being born there or being accepted as a member by law

permanent resident (noun)
> a person who can live in and work in a country, but is not a citizen

1. One reason that a person might want to become a citizen instead of a permanent resident is _____

_____

_____

_____

_____

Continue reading the article to find out more about becoming a citizen. Jot down more questions as you read. Look for answers to your questions.

How can someone not born here become a citizen? Here are some things that are necessary. You must be at least 18 years old. You must have been
25   a permanent resident for at least five years. You must be able to speak English. You must also read and write English.

Let's say all of these things fit you. Now there are some steps you must take. First you must fill out an **application.** It asks questions about your **background.**

You also need to get your **fingerprints** taken. Then you need to pass
30   a citizenship test. The test is about U.S. government. It is also about U.S. history.

Finally, you need to see an interviewer. The interviewer listens to why you want to become a citizen and tests your reading and writing skills. Then he or she decides if you will be allowed to become a citizen. If so, you will later take
35   the citizenship oath.

Becoming an American citizen has many benefits . What are they? American citizens can vote in all elections. They can get U.S. passports. Citizens can easily leave the country. They can live in another country for more than two years. Then they can come back whenever they like.
40   Permanent residents can bring husbands, wives, and unmarried children into the U.S. But citizens can bring more relatives to the country. Then these relatives can live here. They will be permanent residents. Citizens can also receive public aid. This includes food stamps.

citizenship (noun)
status of being a citizen

benefits (noun)
things that do something good or give an advantage

2. Four things someone has to do to become a citizen are:

_____

_____

_____

_____

Finish reading the article to see if your questions will be answered.

So now we know why people become citizens. It can be an important step
45   in a person's life. Many people become citizens every year.

July 4 is an important day for Americans. It celebrates a special time. It was
on that day in 1776 that Americans declared themselves free from England.
They did not want to belong to England anymore. They wanted to be their
own country. Each year on July 4 many people become American citizens.
50   On July 4, 2007, about 1,000 people became citizens at Walt Disney World.
There was a special **ceremony** for them. Then they walked down Main Street,
U.S.A. This was an important symbol for the new citizens.

Many people there talked about why they wanted to become citizens.
Many said it was because they wanted to vote. A man named Teddy Alvarez
55   explained why he did it. He said, "Now if I don't like the way things are going,
I can let the government know my opinion." He felt that it was the right thing
to do. He added, "I will always have Mexican blood. But my heart is here."

3. People have ceremonies when they become citizens because _____

_____

_____

_____

_____

_____

_____

4. Do you think people should become American citizens if they can?
    Why or why not?

_____

_____

_____

_____

_____

_____

_____

After You Read

Build a robust vocabulary.

Matching Words   Match the words with their definitions. Write the letter.

_____ 1. process

_____ 2. apply

_____ 3. fingerprints

_____ 4. approved

_____ 5. background

a. allowed or OKed

b. prints made by the pattern of ridges on fingertips

c. to make a formal request

d. a person's experience, education, and family history

e. steps taken to make or do something

Sentence Completions   Complete each sentence using a word from the box.

application	apply	approved	background	ceremony
fingerprints	identification	permission	photograph	process

1. My driver's license is a form of _____.

2. I filled out an _____ for a new job.

3. We need to get _____ to use this room for a party.

4. The school held a _____ for all the graduates.

5. I took a _____ of my whole family together.

Word Building   If a person, place, or thing ends with -*s*, the -*s* often makes the word mean "more than one." Words that mean more than one are called **plurals**. Some words change their spelling when the plural is formed. If a word ends with -*x*, -*ch*, -*sh*, or -*ss*, then you add -*es* to form the plural. For example *splash* becomes *splashes*.

If a word ends with *y*, then you usually change *y* to *i* and add -*es*. For example, *puppy* becomes *puppies*.

Write the plural of each word below.

1. rock: _____

2. fox: _____

3. family: _____

4. word: _____

5. sandal: _____

6. patch: _____

7. baby: _____

8. cross: _____

TIP: If you need to write the plural of a word, look at the ending of the word. Does it end with -ch, -sh, -ss,- x, or -y? If it does, the ending will change when it becomes plural.

Writing Activity Complete this paragraph by using words from the word list on page 55. Reread the definitions, if necessary.

This year I became an American citizen. First I had to fill out an _____.

I had to explain what my _____ was. Then I had to get a set of

_____ taken. It was a long _____, but finally it was over.

There was a special _____ held for new citizens on July 4th.

Think about your reading.

Check your comprehension.   Answer each question. If you don't know the answer, reread the lines in parentheses.

1. What is a green card? (lines 11–16)

    _____

2. What does a citizenship test ask you about? (lines 30–31)

    _____

3. Why do citizens have an easier time leaving the country? (lines 37–39)

    _____

4. What happened on July 4, 1776? (lines 46–47)

    _____

Use reading skills: Compare and contrast.

This article talks about citizens and people who live here but are not citizens. These people are alike in some ways and different in others. When you **compare,** you tell how things are alike. When you **contrast,** you tell how things are different.

Compare and contrast. When you look at details in the article, you can compare and contrast citizens with non-citizens.

> Becoming an American citizen has many benefits. What are they? American citizens can vote in all elections. They can get U.S. passports. Citizens can easily leave the country. They can live in another country for more than two years. Then they can come back whenever they like.

1. Citizens can vote, but non-citizens _____

    _____

    _____

2. Non-citizens cannot get U.S. passports, but citizens _____

    _____

    _____

Use a graphic organizer.

Use the chart below to help you compare and contrast citizens and non-citizens. Fill in the missing infomation.

Citizens	Non-citizens
1. Can vote	Cannot vote
2.	Can bring only husbands, wives, and unmarried children into the country
3. Must speak and read English	

Write About It

Write sentences.

Imagine that you are an adult who has just become an American citizen. Write five sentences that describe what the process was like.

Prewriting   On your own or with a partner, write some details that will help you write your sentences. Fill in the graphic organizer with your ideas. Use as many ovals as you need to fill in the details.

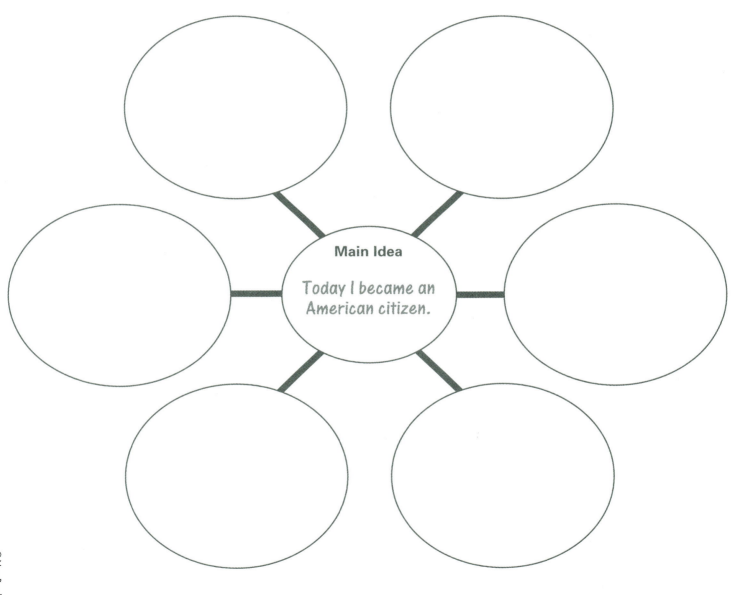

Main Idea

Today I became an American citizen.

Thinking Beyond Reading   Think about these questions and discuss them with a partner. Add ideas to the graphic organizer as you talk.

- Why did you decide to become an American citizen?

- How do you feel now that you are a citizen?

- Why is it important to you?

Write your sentences.   Write your final sentences. Use the ideas in your chart to help you write. Remember that a sentence expresses a complete thought or idea. It always begins with a capital letter. It always ends with a punctuation mark. Usually it ends with a period or a question mark. Sometimes it ends with an exclamation point.

_____

_____

_____

_____

_____

_____

_____

_____

_____

_____

_____

_____

_____

_____

_____

_____

Revise and edit.   Check your sentences for these specific points:

- Did you write in complete sentences?

- Do your sentences relate to each other?

- Did you use correct spelling and punctuation in your sentences?

Learning to Swim

Learning Objectives

In this lesson you will:

▨ Read a story about a man taking his first swimming lesson.

▨ Learn to predict outcomes.

▨ Master the key vocabulary used in the story.

▨ Write sentences that tell what it was like for you to do something for the first time.

Key Vocabulary

aisle *(noun)* an open space to walk between rows

brief *(adjective)* short

conquer *(verb)* to overcome something

dangling *(verb)* hanging loosely

exclaimed *(verb)* said in a loud voice and with strong feeling

glide *(verb)* to move smoothly along something

instructor *(noun)* a person who teaches

nervous *(adjective)* showing or feeling worry or fear

paused *(verb)* stopped for a short time before starting again

suggested *(verb)* told someone what you thought was a good thing to do

Before You Read

When they read, good readers often think about their own experiences. As you read this story, try to think about what you already know about learning to swim. Based on what you know and what you've read, you can also try to predict what will happen.

Use what you know.

1. Some people don't know how to swim because _____

    _____

    _____

    _____

2. It might be hard for an adult to take swimming lessons for the first

    time because _____

    _____

    _____

    _____

    _____

Predict what will happen.

1. The title of the story tells me _____

    _____

    _____

    _____

2. The picture on page 67 shows me _____

    _____

    _____

    _____

    _____

To Sink or Swim

Read the story about a man taking swimming lessons for the first time. Underline words or phrases that help you picture the characters in your mind.

Ken Jackson pushed open the locker room door. He walked along the tiles to where the class waited. They were all sitting on the edge of the pool. Some were **dangling** their feet in the water. The **instructor** was already in the pool and talking to the class.

5   "Hello," she said to Ken. "Are you taking this class, too?"

Ken could barely answer. He looked around at the other six people in the class. Some were definitely older than he was. This made him feel better. "Yes," he said, "I'm Ken." He sat down with the others on the edge of the pool.

"I'm Erica," the instructor told Ken. "I was just saying that we're going to

10 start slowly. But I promise, by the end of these six weeks you will at least go under water!" she said brightly. "Now let's begin. Let's start by getting into the water." The water was colder than Ken had expected. At least it wasn't too deep. He was a tall man and the water was just over his waist.

A woman turned to him and said, "Can't swim, huh?" Before Ken could

15 answer, she said, "Me neither. I've wanted to learn for years and years. I figure 65 isn't too old to learn! What do you think?"

Ken didn't know what to think. It was hard to believe he was really here. He was nearly 30 years old and he couldn't swim. Not even a little. As a kid he had never taken swimming lessons. In the summers he had usually played

20 under an open fire hydrant on his street.

But his daughter Jessica loved to swim. She always wanted Ken to go with her to the community pool. And every summer he had to tell her that he didn't like swimming pools. He said he didn't like the chlorine . That was

fire hydrant *(noun)*
> a large pipe in a street used for getting water to fight fires

chlorine *(noun)*
> a chemical used to keep swimming pools clean

strokes *(noun)*
the repeated movements used in swimming

25 true, of course. But he was also afraid. So here he was, trying to **conquer** his fear. He didn't want to learn any fancy strokes . He just wanted to be able to play with Jessica at the pool without feeling **nervous** about people knocking into him. Once he learned to swim, he would just tell Jessica that the chlorine didn't bother him anymore. That was if he actually learned to swim.

1. Ken wants to learn to swim because _____

_____

_____

_____

Continue reading the story to find out what Ken does. Keep underlining details that help you picture the characters.

goggles *(noun)*
special glasses that protect your eyes

kickboards *(noun)*
floating boards used by beginning swimmers

30 Erica **suggested** to the class that they might want to get some goggles for next week. "Next week!" **exclaimed** one woman about Ken's age. "Just let me get through this first class!" Everyone laughed.

Erica started them off by blowing bubbles. Ken felt foolish, but he tried not to let it show. Then they practiced floating with kickboards . Erica showed them how to **glide** across the pool. Ken made sure to keep his head as far out 35 of the water as he could. He found that he really enjoyed going across the pool with the kickboard.

Then Erica had them practice kicking. She showed Ken how to kick without splashing so much. "You just have to practice," she told him. Ken kicked across the pool. Then someone's foot kicked out at Ken's hands. He felt 40 the kickboard slip from his hands. He felt himself going under. He came out coughing and choking.

"That's all right," said Erica. "You just needed to hold your breath. Why don't you get back on the kickboard? We'll work on breathing later."

But Ken had already moved over to the ladder. He was still coughing as he 45 climbed out of the pool.

"Ken," said Erica. "You're doing fine. You just need to get back in." But it was too late. Without a word, Ken walked past everyone. He grabbed his towel. He was done with swimming. He was going home.

2. Ken came out of the pool because _____

_____

_____

_____

3. I think that Ken will _____

_____

_____

_____

Finish reading the story to find out what Ken does next.

Ken pushed open the locker-room door. This was it. There was no way he
50 could do this. He couldn't believe he had even tried swimming. Well this was
the end of it. He stormed over to his locker.

As Ken reached his locker, he saw a little boy with his father. They were in
the **aisle** between the lockers. The boy was about Jessica's age, maybe a little
younger. They were both wearing bathing suits. The father was holding towels.
55 He reached for the boy's hand and said, "OK, Danny. Let's go swim."

The boy grinned and said, "OK!"

The father saw Ken looking at them and smiled. Ken offered a **brief** smile
in return. But as the father and son walked toward the door to the pool, Ken
frowned. He began opening his locker. Then he **paused.** He sat down on the
60 bench, thinking. Could he really do this thing? It wasn't really fun. But maybe
it could be. People at the community pool always seemed to be having fun.
Jessica could play for hours in there. And wasn't Jessica the reason he was
doing this in the first place?

Ken picked up his towel. He headed across the locker room to the door and
65 pushed it open. He walked across the tiles to where the class was waiting.

4. Ken decided to go back to his swimming class because _____

_____

_____

_____

5. Do you think Ken will learn to swim? Explain.

_____

_____

_____

After You Read

Build a robust vocabulary.

Matching Words   Match the words with their definitions. Write the letter.

_____ 1. dangling

_____ 2. brief

_____ 3. suggested

_____ 4. instructor

_____ 5. exclaimed

a.   said in a loud voice and with strong feeling

b.   hanging loosely

c.   a person who teaches

d.   short

e.   told someone what you thought was a good thing to do

Sentence Completions   Complete each sentence using a word from the box.

aisle	brief	conquer	dangling	exclaimed
glide	instructor	nervous	paused	suggested

1.   I felt _____ meeting my new teacher.

2.   With her new skates, Loretta can _____ across the ice.

3.   The bride and groom walked down the _____.

4.   Ken _____ before jumping into the pool.

5.   I want to _____ my fear of flying.

Word Building   A **root word** is the word from which other words are formed. Letters are added before and/or after the root word to form a new word. For example, the word *like* is the root word in *unlikely*.

Circle the root word in each of the words in the box below.

careless	incomplete	unemployment	reread

Look at the words in the box below. Can you find the root word in each? Circle them.

review	unhappy	rewrite	useful	inconvenient

Circle the root word in each word below. Then use each in a sentence. The first one is done for you.

1. re(view)ed: _We reviewed the lesson before class_____.

2. unhappy: _____

3. rewrite: _____

4. useful: _____

5. inconvenient: _____

TIP: When you read, you may find some long words that you do not recognize. Look closely to see if you recognize the root word. That may help you figure out the meaning of the long word.

Writing Activity Complete this paragraph by using words from the word list on page 65. Reread the definitions, if necessary.

My friend _____ that I take a swimming class. I was

_____, but I decided to try it. My swimming _____

was very helpful. He showed us how to _____ across the water. I think

this class will help me _____ my fear of the water.

Think about your reading.

Check your comprehension.   Answer each question. If you don't know the answer, reread the lines in parentheses.

1. Who is Ken's swimming instructor? (line 9)

   _____

2. What does the instructor suggest everyone bring to the next class? (lines 29–30)

   _____

3. Who does Ken see in the locker room? (lines 52–55)

   _____

4. What does Ken do at the end of the story? (lines 64–65)

   _____

Use reading skills: Predict outcomes.

Sometimes when you are reading, there are clues about what might happen next. You can use these clues to **predict outcomes** in the story.

Predict outcomes.   Read this paragraph from the story. What clues help a reader predict what will happen next?

> Ken Jackson pushed open the locker-room door. He walked along the tiles to where the class waited. They were all sitting on the edge of the pool. Some were dangling their feet in the water. The instructor was already in the pool and talking to the class.

1. The paragraph tells the reader that Ken is walking to _____

_____

2. It also tells the reader that the class is sitting _____

_____

3. These clues tell the reader that the next thing Ken will probably do is _____

_____

Use a graphic organizer.

Fill in the missing information in the chart below.

Clue	What You Can Predict
1. Ken is nervous about taking swimming lessons.	He'll go to class because he wants to swim with his daughter.
2. Ken likes using the kickboard.	
3. Ken gets knocked underwater.	
4. Ken sees a father and son in the locker room and thinks about Jessica.	

Write About It

Write sentences.

Do you remember a time when you did something for the first time? Maybe it was riding a bicycle or driving a car. Think about what the experience was like. Write five sentences that describe your experience.

Prewriting On your own or with a partner, write ideas that will help you remember exactly what happened. Think about the steps you followed and the order in which you followed them. Also think about how you felt during each step. Fill in the graphic organizer with your ideas.

Steps	How I Felt
1.	
2.	
3.	
4.	
5.	

Thinking Beyond Reading   Think about these questions and discuss them with a partner. Add ideas to the graphic organizer as you talk.

- What did you do?

- Who helped you?

- What were the steps you followed?

- How did you feel as you went through the steps?

Write your sentences.   Write your final sentences. Use the ideas in your chart to help you write. Remember that a sentence expresses a complete thought or idea. It always begins with a capital letter. It always ends with a punctuation mark. Usually it ends with a period or a question mark. Sometimes it ends with an exclamation point.

_____

_____

_____

_____

_____

_____

_____

_____

_____

_____

_____

_____

_____

Revise and edit.   Check your sentences for these points:

- Did you write in complete sentences?

- Do your sentences relate to each other?

- Did you use correct spelling and punctuation in your sentences?

Transportation Troubles

Learning Objectives

In this lesson you will:

◼ Read a story about a man who must find a way to get to work when he can't take the bus.

◼ Learn to make inferences.

◼ Master the key vocabulary used in the story.

◼ Write sentences that tell about how you would get to work if your usual means of transportation were not available.

Key Vocabulary

afford *(verb)* to have enough money for; to be able to pay for

challenge *(noun)* an interesting or difficult problem

emerged *(verb)* came out into view

exhausted *(adjective)* tired; worn out

gestured *(verb)* used the body, face, or hands to communicate

interrupted *(verb)* broke in or cut off someone who was speaking

rummaging *(verb)* searching for something by moving things around

site *(noun)* a place; a location

transportation *(noun)* the act of moving things or people from one place to another

unfortunately *(adverb)* marked by bad luck

Before You Read

Before you read the story, you know it's about getting to work. Think about how you get to work or school. What would happen if you couldn't do that? Think about what you might learn from reading the story.

Set a purpose for reading.

1. The title and the picture tell me _____

_____

_____

_____

THINK ABOUT IT

The title makes me think about how I get to the places I go. What if something happened and I had to change?

2. This story interests me because _____

_____

_____

_____

_____

Use what you know.

1. I usually get to work by _____

_____

_____

_____

THINK ABOUT IT

Sometimes if there's a problem with the trains, I have to wait a long time. This makes me late for work. Sometimes I wonder what I'd do if the train didn't come at all.

2. It would be a problem if buses or trains were not working in the

morning because _____

_____

_____

_____

_____

How Many Ways to Get to Work?

Read the following story about a man who has to find a new way to get to work. Highlight or mark clues in the story that tell you how the characters are feeling.

Lou Ramirez unlocked the door to his apartment. He was **exhausted.** It was late. His girlfriend Rosa was waiting for him in the living room. "What happened?" said Rosa, jumping up. "You're two hours late!"

Lou sighed. "I have to sit down. I was waiting for that bus for over an hour! 5 And I had to stand all the way. The bus drivers are probably going on strike . So there aren't too many buses running even now. That's what happened!"

"Oh, no!" said Rosa. "A bus strike? What are you going to do? How are you going to get to work?" Rosa worked as a receptionist in an office not far away. She usually enjoyed the short walk to work. The winters could be tough 10 sometimes, but she managed. There was no way, however, that Lou could walk to work. It would take him hours.

"I just wish we had a car," said Lou.

"Lou," said Rosa, "we can't **afford** a car and you know it. The buses are usually fine. And the strike will be over soon, I bet. Hey, couldn't you ask 15 someone to drive—"

"No, Rosa," Lou **interrupted.** "I'm not going to ask someone to go out of their way. No one really lives near us. It would just be too much. I have to think of something else. They really seem serious about the strike. There might be no buses at all tomorrow."

20 "Well," said Rosa. "We have to think of something. Why don't you have some dinner, and then we can talk about it some more?"

strike *(noun)*
a stopping of work as a protest for better pay or working conditions

receptionist *(noun)*
a person whose job is to greet people and answer the telephone

"Rosa, I don't want to talk about it. I don't even want to think about it," said Lou, heading over to the stove. "Let me just have some of this rice."

1. If I took the bus to work and the buses weren't going to be running,

    I'd feel _____

    _____

    _____

Continue reading the story to see what Lou decides to do. Highlight or mark phrases that give clues about the characters.

After dinner, Rosa said, "OK, are you ready to talk about the bus strike
25   again? Because I think I have the answer. What about your bike?"
"My bike?"
"Yes," said Rosa, "your bike. It's just sitting in the back of our closet collecting dust! Why don't you take it to work?"
"No, that's not a good idea. I don't know—"
30   "But it makes sense, right, Lou? It wouldn't take you that long."
"Rosa," said Lou. "I don't want to show up for work on a bike!"
"Why not?" said Rosa. "What's the big deal?"
"It's just not—besides, I don't even know if it's still got good tires or anything." Lou glanced over at the closet, thinking about it.
35   Rosa said, "OK, Lou, it's up to you. But I just don't know how you're going to get to work."
The next morning, Lou got up an hour earlier than usual. "I'm going to check out the buses," he said to Rosa. "I have to see if they're really on strike."
"OK," said Rosa, getting out of bed. "I'll be here when you come back in
40   five minutes!"
"Very funny!" said Lou. "Don't count on it!" But **unfortunately** he was back in five minutes. "Don't say anything," he said, as rushed back in the door. He headed straight to the closet and started **rummaging** through it. He **emerged** a moment later with a bicycle.
45   Rosa smiled as Lou tested the tires. "So do you think it's OK to get to work by bicycle?" she asked.
"Do I have any choice?" Lou said, angrily. "I'll see you later!" He pushed his bicycle out the door.

2. Lou decided to take his bike to work because _____

    _____

    _____

Finish reading the article to find out how Lou feels about riding his bike to work.

Lou set out for work. He was working downtown on a construction **site**
50 for the whole month. He was sure no one else would be using a bicycle
for **transportation.**

As Lou set out, he felt angry. But as he rode along, he began to feel better.
He had forgotten how much he'd liked riding his bike. Riding his bike through
the city streets was a **challenge,** but he enjoyed it.

55 By the time he reached the construction site, he felt pretty good. Maybe
this bus strike wasn't such a bad thing after all. He could ride a bike for a day or
two, even a few weeks if he had to.

Lou locked his bike to a parking meter across the street. He waited outside
the building for a while and then saw the job foreman .

60 "Hey, Jerry," said Lou, "am I the only one here?"

"Looks like it," said his boss. "It's this bus strike, you know. But people
better start showing up soon is all I can say!"

At the end of the long day, Lou was heading across the street to unlock
his bike.

65 "Hey, Lou," shouted someone. "Where are you going?"

Lou just **gestured** across the street, hoping that was enough.

"Oh man, you rode a bike here?" said Francisco, seeing where Lou was
going.

"Yeah," said Lou, "so what?"

70 Before anyone said anything else, Jerry stepped in. "Hey, Lou was the only
guy who got here on time today. I wouldn't be laughing so hard if I were you.
Know what I mean?"

Francisco said, "Hey, I was only thinking that it was probably, you know,
kind of fun riding a bike through the city."

75 Lou shrugged. "It was all right," he said. But as he turned his head so no
one could see, he had a big grin on his face.

meter (noun)
a device that measures or records time, distance, speed, quantity, or degree

foreman (noun)
the person in charge of a work crew

3. Lou decided that riding a bike to work was fine because _____

_____

_____

4. Do you think Lou will continue riding his bike to work even after the buses
start running again? Why or why not?

_____

_____

_____

After You Read

Build a robust vocabulary.

Matching Words   Match the words with their definitions. Write the letter.

_____ 1. emerged

_____ 2. rummaging

_____ 3. challenge

_____ 4. unfortunately

_____ 5. gestured

a.   marked by bad luck

b.   an interesting or difficult problem

c.   came out into view

d.   searching for something by moving things around

e.   used the body, face, or hands to communicate

Sentence Completions   Complete each sentence using a word from the box.

afford	challenge	emerged	exhausted	gestured
interrupted	rummaging	site	transportation	unfortunately

1.   They're building a factory on this _____.

2.   What type of _____ do you use to get to work?

3.   He _____ me as I was talking.

4.   I don't think we can _____ a new car.

5.   She felt _____ at the end of the long day.

Word Building   Look at the following words. What do you notice about all of these words?

airplane	lawnmower	highchair	cookbook

Each word is a made up of two smaller words. The longer words are **compound words.**

Draw a line between the two parts of each word. Compare your answers with a partner. Discuss what each word means. Use the meaning of each part of the word to help you define the word.

Read these compound words. What is the same about all of these words? What does *under* mean in these words? Write the meaning of each word on the line next to it.

1. underground: _____

2. underwater: _____

3. undershirt: _____

4. underline: _____

TIP: When you read, you may find some long words that you do not recognize. Does the word have two words combined to make one word? Look closely to see if the word is a compound word.

Writing Activity   Complete this paragraph by using words from the word list on page 75. Reread the definitions, if necessary.

What kind of _____ do you take to get to work? I usually take the bus,

but _____ it's not running today. Now it will be a _____

to get to work. I can't _____ to rent a car. I feel _____

just thinking about this!

Think about your reading.

Check your comprehension.   Answer each question. If you don't know the answer, reread the lines in parentheses.

1. Why was Lou late getting home from work? (lines 4–6)

_____

2. What does Rosa suggest Lou use to get to work? (lines 24–25)

_____

3. Where does Lou lock his bicycle? (line 58)

_____

4. Why was Lou the only person to get to work on time? (lines 61–62)

_____

Use reading skills: Make inferences.

Authors don't always tell you everything you need to know in a story. Sometimes they give you clues. You can use these clues and what you already know to make good guesses, or **inferences,** about story events or characters.

Make inferences. You can make inferences by completing each of the following sentences.

1. Lou tells Rosa he doesn't want to take his bicycle to work because _____

   _____

2. When Lou has to take his bike to work, he locks it up across the street because _____

   _____

3. We can infer that Lou does not want to bike to work because _____

   _____

Use a graphic organizer.

Fill in the missing information in the chart below.

Story Clues	+	What I Know	=	Inference
Lou is late getting home from work because his bus was late.		When there is a problem with transportation, you might be late.		1. Lou can't count on his usual _____.
Lou's bike is collecting dust in the closet.		If something is buried in a closet, you don't use it much.		2. Lou last rode his bike _____.
Francisco asks Lou how he got to work.		It's always good to get to work on time.		3. When Francisco finds out that Lou was the only one who got to work on time Francisco feels _____.

Write About It

Write sentences.

How do you get to work? What if your usual way of getting to work was not possible? Suppose your car broke down or the trains stopped running. What would you do? Write five sentences that describe what you can do instead.

Prewriting   On your own or with a partner, write some ideas that will help you write your sentences. Fill in the graphic organizer with your ideas.

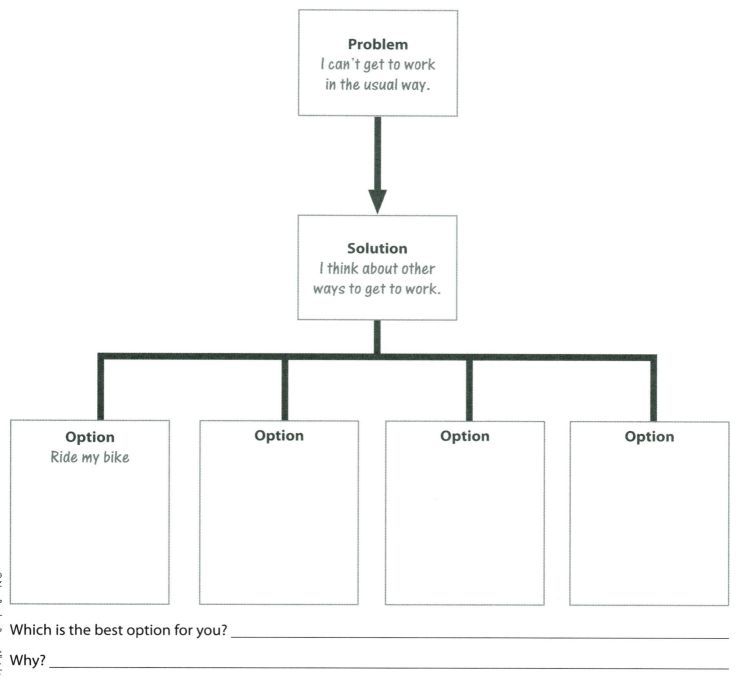

Problem
I can't get to work
in the usual way.

Solution
I think about other
ways to get to work.

Option
Ride my bike

Option

Option

Option

Which is the best option for you? _____

Why? _____

Thinking Beyond Reading   Think about these questions and discuss them with a partner. Add ideas to the graphic organizer as you talk.

- How do you get to work?

- What are other ways you might get to work?

- What is the best way if you can't get to work as you usually do?

Write your sentences.   Write your final sentences. Use the ideas in your chart to help you write. Remember that a sentence expresses a complete thought or idea. It always begins with a capital letter. It always ends with a punctuation mark. Usually it ends with a period or a question mark. Sometimes it ends with an exclamation point.

_____

_____

_____

_____

_____

_____

_____

_____

_____

_____

_____

_____

_____

_____

Revise and edit.   Check your sentences for these points:

- Did you write in complete sentences?

- Do your sentences relate to each other?

- Did you use correct spelling and punctuation in your sentences?

Food for Thought

Learning Objectives

In this lesson you will:

■ Read a story about a woman who uses her grandmother's cookie recipe.

■ Learn to identify time order.

■ Master the key vocabulary used in the story.

■ Write sentences that tell about a time when you made something good to eat.

Key Vocabulary

anticipation *(noun)* the act of looking forward to something

aroma *(noun)* a strong, usually pleasant, smell

batch *(noun)* an amount of something made at one time

batter *(noun)* a mixture of flour, eggs, and liquid

burst *(verb)* entered suddenly

handwriting *(noun)* the way someone writes

ingredients *(noun)* the parts of a mixture

recipe *(noun)* a list of foods and instructions for cooking something

rejected *(noun)* refused to accept or approve

satisfied *(adjective)* happy with what you have, needing nothing else

Before You Read

Good readers often make connections to what they know as they read. Sometimes they try to predict what a story will be about. Both of these active reading strategies can help you understand this story about a woman using her grandmother's recipe.

Use what you know.

1. People like to use recipes from their relatives because _____

_____

_____

_____

_____

My mother's chicken soup is so good. I know she adds a lot of vegetables to it. I wish I could make chicken soup as good as hers.

2. I wish I had the recipe for _____

_____

_____

_____

_____

Make predictions.

1. When I look at the picture and read the title, I think the story will be

about _____

_____

_____

_____

_____

When I use my mother's recipes, I remember how she taught me to cook. I wonder if the woman in the story will feel the same way when she uses her grandmother's recipe.

The Right Recipe

Read the story about a woman who gets her grandmother's cookie recipe. Underline words or phrases that will help you predict what comes next in the story.

On Friday evening, Tina Ucci **burst** into her apartment. "Guess what!" she shouted to her husband Dan. He was sitting on the couch watching TV. "I have Grandma Ucci's **recipe** for her famous biscotti ! Can you believe it?"

"How did you get that?" said Dan, looking up briefly from the TV.

5 "Well," began Tina. "I was at Aunt Adela's house. She was going through all these papers that Grandma left when she died. And there was the recipe in Grandma's beautiful **handwriting.** Aunt Adela made me a copy. I can't wait to get started baking. I really miss Grandma's biscotti."

The next evening Tina got out the recipe. It didn't seem very hard. She
10 had needed to buy a few things, like almond extract . But she already had most of the **ingredients** at home.

First she measured out the dry ingredients. She got out flour. She got out salt. She got out baking powder. She put them in a large bowl. Then she mixed them together. She got out a second bowl. She put in some sugar and eggs. She
15 mixed them together. Next she added vanilla and almond extract. Then she added chopped nuts. She glanced at the recipe.

"Oh, I need to grate some orange peel! Do we have a grater in the house?" she called out to Dan.

"A grater?" Dan called back.

20 Tina sighed. "OK, I guess I can just use a knife. Maybe if I chop it up really tiny?"

"Well, what did your grandmother use?" said Dan, coming into the kitchen.

biscotti *(noun)*
a crisp Italian cookie

extract *(noun)*
a concentrated flavoring used in cooking

grater *(noun)*
a kitchen tool used to shred food

spatula (noun)
a kitchen tool used for
mixing and spreading

25 "She used a grater. Grandma was always grating orange and lemon peels for things. I wish I had Grandma's grater." Tina worked with a knife. She tried to scrape the peel off an orange. She added the peel to the second bowl. Then she stirred the mixture with a spatula . Finally she added the dry ingredients to the second bowl. She stirred them in.

"Now I just have to split the **batter** in half and bake the halves like loaves of bread."

30 "Are you sure that's right?" said Dan.

"That's what it says here," said Tina, pointing to the paper.

"Did she really write about loaves of bread?" asked Dan, looking uncertain.

"Well, no, Aunt Adela told me about that part. See, when it's done baking, you cut the loaves into slices. Then you have cookies. But then
35 you have to bake them for a second time. The second time is just for a few minutes."

"How many minutes?" asked Dan.

"I don't know. Grandma didn't say. It just says to bake it a second time."

1. I think Tina's biscotti will turn out to be _____

_____

_____

Continue reading the story to find out how Tina's biscotti turn out. See if you can predict what will happen next.

Tina popped the loaves into the oven. After about ten minutes, a delicious
40 **aroma** filled the kitchen. Suddenly Tina's son Christopher burst out of his room. "What's that amazing smell?" he asked, racing into the kitchen.

"It's biscotti," Tina said, smiling. "My grandma's famous recipe. But you have to wait." Tina was filled with **anticipation.** Finally it was time to take the loaves out of the oven. Tina cut them into slices. Then she put them back in
45 the oven. She waited about ten minutes. The cookies were golden brown. She took them out of the oven again. When they cooled down, she offered some to Christopher and Dan.

Christopher took a big bite. Then he smiled. "It's great, Mom. It's really great."
50 "Yeah Tina, I love it," said Dan, smiling, too.

Tina had a big smile on her face as she took a bite. Suddenly her smile faded. "This doesn't taste like Grandma's."

"That doesn't matter," said Dan. "They're really good."

But Tina had already **rejected** the cookies. "What do you know?" snapped
55 Tina. She stormed out of the kitchen.

2. Tina is unhappy because _____

_____

_____

3. Now I think Tina is going to _____

_____

_____

Finish reading the story to see if your prediction is correct.

Tina felt terrible. She tried to make a second **batch** of biscotti, but she still wasn't **satisfied.** So she called Aunt Adela. She tried to hold herself together. But the minute she heard Adela's voice she started to cry. "I tried to make Grandma's biscotti. They taste good. But they don't taste like Grandma's."

60 "That is so like your grandma," said Adela, chuckling. "She probably left something out of the recipe so that no one could make their biscotti taste like hers."

"What? You think she really did that? You don't think I did anything wrong?"

65 "Of course not. But Tina, did anyone like them?"

"Well yeah, Dan and Christopher loved them. But of course, they never had Grandma's famous biscotti."

Adela said, "Well now they're Tina's famous biscotti. Did you like them?"

"Yeah," said Tina.

70 "So you see," said Adela. "That recipe was for your grandma's biscotti. But this recipe is for your biscotti. Every recipe is yours once you make it. Do you see?"

"I guess," said Tina. "I still miss Grandma, though."

"We all do," said Adela. "But now you can think of her every time you

75 make these cookies."

4. Tina felt better after talking to her aunt because _____

_____

_____

5. Why do you think Tina's cookies were not the same as her grandmother's cookies?

_____

_____

After You Read

Build a robust vocabulary.

Matching Words   Match the words with their definitions. Write the letter.

_____ 1. burst

_____ 2. rejected

_____ 3. batch

_____ 4. aroma

_____ 5. anticipation

a. entered suddenly

b. the act of looking forward to something

c. an amount of something made at one time

d. a strong, usually pleasant, smell

e. refused to accept or approve

Sentence Completions   Complete each sentence using a word from the box.

anticipation	aroma	batch	batter	burst
handwriting	ingredients	recipe	rejected	satisfied

1. I have an excellent _____ for making apple pie.

2. It was easy to read the teacher's _____ on the board.

3. Chris poured the _____ into the cake pan and put it in the oven.

4. We don't have all the _____ for this pie.

5. Patty was _____ with the way her cake came out.

Word Building   There are many prefixes in English. When you add a prefix to a word, you change the meaning. For example, the prefix *re-* means "again." The word *rewind* means "to wind again." Look at the chart below. It shows some common prefixes and their meanings.

Prefix	Meaning	Example
pre-	before	prereading
dis-	not	disconnect
non-	without	nonviolent
anti-	against	antisocial
inter-	between	international

Look at these words. Underline the prefix in each word.

| preview | dislike | nonstop | preheat |

Match the prefix in the first column with the correct word in the second column. Write the new word in the third column. The first one is done for you.

1. pre-   traditional   _prepay_____

2. dis-   comfort   _____

3. non-   pay   _____

4. inter-   freeze   _____

5. anti-   office   _____

TIP: You may be able to use what you know about prefixes to tell what an unknown word means. For example, knowing the prefix *re-* means "again" will help you understand that *replay* means "play again."

Writing Activity   Complete this paragraph by using words from the word list on page 85. Reread the definitions, if necessary.

My friend gave me a great _____ for chocolate cake. First I got all the

_____. Then I mixed everything and poured the _____

into a cake pan. When it was done, the kitchen was filled with a wonderful

_____. I was very _____ with my chocolate cake.

Think about your reading.

Check your comprehension.   Answer each question. If you don't know the answer, reread the lines in parentheses.

1. What does Tina get a recipe for? (line 3)

_____

2. What does Tina need that she doesn't have? (lines 17–18)

_____

3. Who are the first people to try Tina's cookies? (lines 46–47)

_____

4. Who is the last person that Tina talks to? (lines 74–75)

_____

Use reading skills: Identify time order.

Articles and stories are sometimes arranged by the order of events. When you read, you can look for words that identify **time order.** Some words that give clues to time order are *first, second, then, later, before, after,* and *finally.*

Identify time order.   Read the following sentences from the story. Each sentence contains one or more words that tell when an event happened. Underline those words in each sentence.

1.   The next evening, Tina got out the recipe.

2.   First she measured out the dry ingredients.

3.   Next she added vanilla and almond extract.

4.   After about ten minutes, a delicious smell filled the kitchen.

5.   Finally it was time to take the loaves out of the oven.

Use a graphic organizer.

Read the paragraph below. Then fill in the chart telling what happened. Use the correct time order and words such as *first, then, later, next, last,* and *finally.*

> Tina measured out the ingredients. She put them in a large bowl. She mixed them together. She added more ingredients. She put the cookies into the oven.

Steps
1. First Tina measured out the ingredients.
2.
3.
4.
5.

Write About It

Write sentences.

Think about a time that you made something that tasted really good. It could be something complicated that required a recipe. It could be something easy, like a sandwich, but it should have at least 5 steps. Write five sentences that tell the steps you took when making this food.

Prewriting On your own or with a partner, write ideas that will help you remember exactly what happened. Think about the steps you followed and the order in which you followed them. Fill in the graphic organizer with your ideas.

Steps
1.
2.
3.
4.
5.

Suppose you did something out of order. What would have happened?

_____

_____

_____

_____

Thinking Beyond Reading   Think about these questions and discuss them with a partner. Add ideas to the graphic organizer as you talk.

- What did you make?

- What was the first thing you did?

- What were the next steps?

- What was the last thing you did?

- What decisions did you have to make while you were making it?

Write your sentences.   Write your final sentences. Use the details in your chart to help you write. Remember that a sentence expresses a complete thought or idea. It always begins with a capital letter. It always ends with a punctuation mark. Usually it ends with a period or a question mark. Sometimes it ends with an exclamation point.

_____

_____

_____

_____

_____

_____

_____

_____

_____

_____

_____

_____

_____

Revise and edit.   Check your sentences for these points:

- Did you write in complete sentences?

- Do your sentences relate to each other?

- Did you use correct spelling and punctuation in your sentences?

Trading Clothes, Saving Money

Learning Objectives

In this lesson you will:

◼ Learn about a way to trade old clothes for new ones.

◼ Learn to synthesize information.

◼ Master the key vocabulary used in the article.

◼ Write sentences that tell what it might be like to go to a clothing swap.

Key Vocabulary

admission *(noun)* a fee paid for entry

concept *(noun)* a thought or idea

fee *(noun)* an amount of money charged for a service

full-length *(adjective)* showing the whole human figure

informal *(adjective)* casual; not formal

manages *(verb)* directs or controls

opportunity *(noun)* a good chance to do something

recycle *(verb)* reuse

swap *(noun)* an exchange of one thing for another

variety *(noun)* a number of different things

Before You Read

As you begin to read the article, you will see that it mentions having clothing at home that you never wear. Think about what you already know about this topic and what you would like to find out as you read.

Use what you know.

THINK ABOUT IT

1. Many people have clothing they never wear because _____

   _____

   _____

   _____

Once I bought a dress for my sister's wedding. I never wore it again. Now it just hangs in my closet!

2. An item of clothing that I have and never wear is _____

   _____

   _____

   _____

Set a purpose for reading.

THINK ABOUT IT

1. The title of the article tells me that it will be about _____

   _____

   _____

   _____

I've always wondered what to do with clothes I don't need anymore. Maybe this article will give me some ideas.

2. I will read this article in order to find out _____

   _____

   _____

   _____

Old Clothes For New

Read the following article to learn about clothing swaps. Underline important words that help you understand key ideas about the topic.

Do you have clothes you never wear? Maybe you have pants that don't fit. Or a dress shirt you wore only once. You probably have clothes you bought a long time ago. Now they just sit in your closet. But what if you could trade them for something else? What if you ended up with a bunch of new clothes?
5   It's very easy to do this. This is what happens at a clothing **swap.**

Just picture a room full of friends. Everyone has bags of clothes that they no longer want. People dump out their bags. Then everyone goes through the clothes. They find things they like. It works out for everyone. You end up with new clothes. Plus you get rid of your old ones. Your old clothes become
10   someone's new clothes. And no one spends any money.

This is not a new **concept.** Parents have been doing this for years. Many parents hand down clothes that their children have outgrown to friends or relatives. They might get clothes in return. It makes sense because it saves money. And it's a great way to **recycle** old clothes.
15   Now clothing swaps have become a trend all over the country. They used to happen in people's homes. But now people also have them in public places. These include bars and community centers. That way, anyone is welcome.

Men and women come in with bags of old clothes. They go through other piles of clothes. Then they take as much as they want. Usually there are no
20   changing rooms at clothing swaps. People just try things on over their own clothes. Then they can ask their friends what they think.

trend *(noun)*
a current style or fashion

1. So far, the article has told me that clothing swaps _____

_____

_____

_____

_____

Continue reading the article to find out how having a clothing swap can make you money. Keep underlining key ideas in the article.

The idea for clothing swaps first started with women. Now plenty of men go to them, too. As one woman put it, "Guys don't like to shop, and they don't like to spend money for clothes. So they come here and they get free stuff!"

25 Some clothing swaps have rules. Some ask that clothes be cleaned or pressed. Some just ask that clothes be in good condition. Most clothing swaps are free. Yet some charge a small **fee** to cover certain costs. This might include renting the space.

Some people have used clothing swaps as a business **opportunity.** If you 30 charge **admission,** you can end up making money. People pay to get in. But all the clothes are free. And you don't have to provide anything but the space. So it's not too hard to make a profit .

profit (noun)
the amount of money made in a business that is more than the amount put in

2. People sometimes charge money to enter clothing swaps because

_____

_____

_____

_____

Finish reading the article to find out how to have your own clothing swap.

But maybe you want to try something more **informal.** You could start with a clothing swap at your house. Invite a group of friends. You can ask your 35 friends to invite their friends. This might give you a better **variety** of clothes. Make sure you have at least two **full-length** mirrors. That way people can try on clothes and see how they look.

Decide what to do if two people want the same thing. That can happen fairly often. You might decide to flip a coin. And you don't have to limit 40 yourself to just clothes. You can include shoes. You can also have accessories and jewelry.

accessories (noun)
things that you add to something else to make it nicer or better

Many people like the idea of clothing swaps. Sally Newman **manages** a clothing swap. She points out that often you have to convince people to keep a new idea going. But everybody already thinks this is a good idea. So there's not a lot that has to be done. People will keep going to clothing swaps. You will find more of them all over the country. It looks like they are here for good.

What happens to the stuff no one wants? At the end of the swap, there is usually some clothing left over. Often it is taken to a thrift shop . So that clothing will also end up going somewhere. You can be sure that someone will wear it someday.

And what if you decide you don't like something you got at a clothing swap? Just bring it to the next clothing swap!

thrift shop *(noun)*
a shop that sells used articles, especially clothes

3. The best thing about a clothing swap is _____

_____

_____

_____

_____

_____

4. Would you like to have a clothing swap? Why or why not?

_____

_____

_____

_____

_____

After You Read

Build a robust vocabulary.

Matching Words   Match the words in the first column with the correct definitions in the second column.

_____ 1. concept   a.   not formal

_____ 2. fee   b.   an exchange of one thing for another

_____ 3. informal   c.   a thought or idea

_____ 4. opportunity   d.   an amount of money charged for a service

_____ 5. swap   e.   a good chance to do something

Sentence Completions   Complete each sentence using a word from the box.

admission	concept	fee	full-length	informal
manages	opportunity	recycle	swap	variety

1.   She _____ a restaurant.

2.   There is a _____ of clothing to look at.

3.   The movie theater charges $9 for _____.

4.   We can _____ these bottles after they're empty.

5.   I'd like to see this dress in the _____ mirror.

Word Building   A **suffix** is a group of letters added to the end of a word. When a suffix is added, a new word with a new meaning is formed. The suffix *-ness* means the "condition of." *Happiness* is the condition of being happy.

Read these words. Each word ends with a suffix. Draw a circle around the suffix in each word.

sadness	joyfulness	hopelessness	foolishness

| loudness | brightness | sleepiness | soreness |

Complete each sentence below by choosing a word that ends with the suffix *-ness*.

1. The _____ of the light bothered my eyes.

2. _____ came over her as the clock reached midnight.

3. Exercise sometimes causes _____ in your muscles.

4. This switch controls _____, or volume.

TIP: When you come across a word you do not know, see if the word has a suffix, or ending, you recognize such as *-ness* in *happiness.* If you know what the suffix means, you may be able to figure out the meaning of the word.

Writing Activity Complete this paragraph by using words from the word list on page 95. Reread the definitions, if necessary.

I'm going to a clothing _____. It's a good way to

_____ old clothes. Sometimes you need to pay a small

_____ to get in. There is usually a good _____ of clothes

there. I think it's also a great _____ to meet people and get new clothes.

Think about your reading.

Check your comprehension. Answer each question. If you don't know the answer, reread the lines in parentheses.

1. What is a clothing swap? **(lines 5–10)**

_____

2. Why would people charge a fee at a clothing swap? **(lines 27–28)**

_____

3. Where could you hold an informal clothing swap? **(lines 33–34)**

_____

4. What usually happens to the stuff that no one wants at a clothing swap? **(lines 48–49)**

_____

Use reading skills: Synthesize information.

When you **synthesize** information, you add new information to something you already know.
Then you come up with a new idea or a new understanding.

Synthesize information.   When you complete the following, you can put together
what you already know with what you learned to come up with a new idea.

1. Something you already know.
   List some things you have in your closet besides clothes that you don't wear or no longer need.

   _____

   _____

2. Something you learned from the article.
   List some things that clothing swaps also include.

   _____

   _____

3. Synthesize.
   Put together the information from the two lists above to come up with a new idea. Write the new idea.

   _____

   _____

Use a graphic organizer.

Fill in the missing information in the chart below. The first one is done for you.

Something I Know	What I Learned	New Idea
1. I have clothes that I never wear.	People trade clothing at clothing swaps.	I can get rid of clothes I don't want and get something I do want at a clothing swap.
2. My children outgrow their clothes fast.		
3. I would like to make some extra money.		

Write About It

Write sentences.

Imagine that you are going to a clothing swap. Write five sentences that describe your experience.

Prewriting   On your own or with a partner, use the graphic organizer to help you write your sentences. Write answers in the ovals with questions. Fill in the blank oval with more ideas.

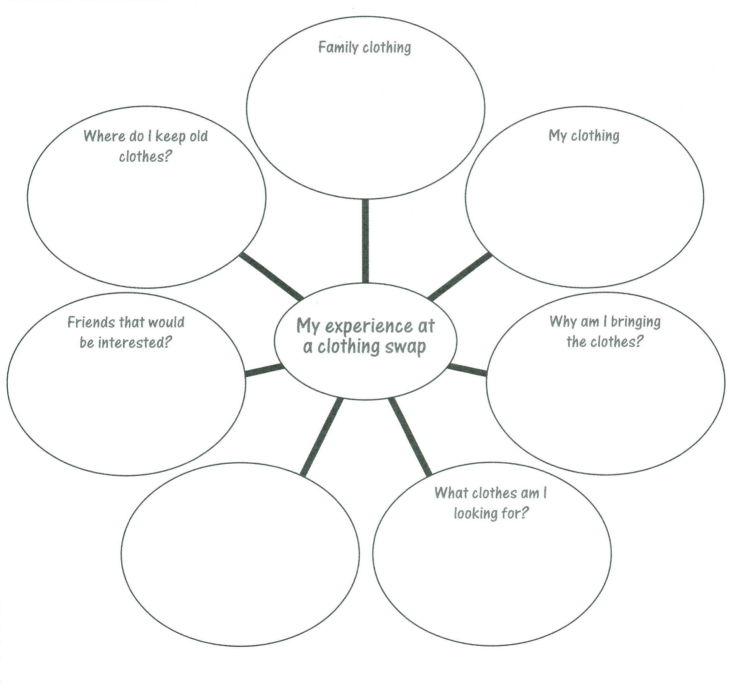

Thinking Beyond Reading   Think about these questions and discuss them with a partner. Add ideas to the graphic organizer as you talk.

- What clothing would you take to the clothing swap?

- What clothing would you look for?

- Which friends or family would be interested?

Write your sentences.   Write your final sentences. Use the details in your chart to help you write. Remember that a sentence expresses a complete thought or idea. It always begins with a capital letter. It always ends with a punctuation mark. Usually it ends with a period or a question mark. Sometimes it ends with an exclamation point.

_____

_____

_____

_____

_____

_____

_____

_____

_____

_____

_____

_____

_____

_____

_____

Revise and edit.   Check your sentences for these points:

- Did you write in complete sentences?

- Do your sentences relate to each other?

- Did you use correct spelling and punctuation in your sentences?

Answer Key

Lesson 1 Good Sleep for Good Health
pp. 5–14

Matching Words
1. b
2. c
3. a
4. d
5. e

Sentence Completions
1. exhausted
2. substitute
3. temporary
4. stress
5. avoid

Word Building
Circle -s or -es in each word.
2. apples
3. desks
4. bunches
5. bosses

Writing Activity
stress

disrupt

exhausted

function

avoid

Check your comprehension.
Sample answers:
1. 7 or 8 hours
2. a few weeks or for months
3. It can cause you to wake up a lot.
4. It can block out noise.

Identify cause and effect.
Sample answers:
1. if someone is in pain
2. he or she won't be able to sleep

Use a graphic organizer.
Sample answers:
2. It blocks out the light.
3. It keeps her from falling asleep.
4. She has a hard time going to sleep on time on Sunday night.

Prewriting
Answers will vary.

Thinking Beyond Reading
Answers will vary.

Write your sentences.
Use the details in your chart to help you write.

Revise and edit.
Sentences should be complete and use correct spelling and punctuation.

Lesson 2 A New Way to Work
pp. 15–24

Matching Words
1. e
2. c
3. d
4. b
5. a

Sentence Completions
1. skilled
2. afford
3. expensive
4. mechanic
5. computer

Word Building
Underline *friend* in each word.

Circle *view* in each word.
1. viewing
2. preview

Writing Activity

expensive

factory

afford

unskilled

technology

Check your comprehension.

Sample answers:

1. in 1903

2. the assembly line

3. three minutes

4. to run some machines

Classify information.

Sample answers:

1. skilled workers

2. unskilled workers

3. did good work

Use a graphic organizer.

Sample answers:

Skilled workers: mechanics, carpenters, drivers, teachers

Unskilled workers: laborers, stock persons, farm workers, plumber's assistants

Prewriting

Answers will vary.

Thinking Beyond Reading

Answers will vary.

Write your sentences.

Use the details in your chart to help you write.

Revise and edit.

Sentences should be complete and use correct spelling and punctuation.

Lesson 3 A Family Visit pp. 25–34

Matching Words

1. c

2. e

3. b

4. d

5. a

Sentence Completions

1. relatives

2. cramped

3. patient

4. scattered

5. glanced

Word Building

Circle *un-* in each word.

2. unwilling

3. unnecessary

4. unopened

5. unlikely

Writing Activity

relatives

recognized

cramped

anxious

obvious

Check your comprehension.

Sample answers:

1. her cousins Juan and Marisol

2. Puerto Rico

3. She is pregnant.

4. making dinner

Make judgments.

Sample answers:

1. good because she was helping them out

2. realistic because they have a small apartment

3. Lizette

4. She knew their apartment was too small, but she was happy to have them stay in the end.

Use a graphic organizer.

Sample answers:

2. It makes sense because their apartment is so small.

3. Her cousins are trying to be good guests.

Prewriting

Answers will vary.

Thinking Beyond Reading

Answers will vary.

Write your sentences.

Use the details in your chart to help you write.

Revise and edit.

Sentences should be complete and use correct spelling and punctuation.

Lesson 4 Connecting a Community
pp. 35–44

Matching Words

1. c

2. b

3. e

4. a

5. d

Sentence Completions

1. information

2. assistant

3. teenage

4. local

5. web site

Word Building

Circle -ful or -ly in each word.

1. helpful

2. slowly

Writing Activity

community

volunteers

information

local

web site

represent

Check your comprehension.

Sample answers:

1. on a bridge in Frederick, Maryland

2. What object best represents the spirit of community to you?

3. two clasped hands

4. thousands

Draw conclusions.

Sample answers:

1. giving ideas about what to paint on the bridge

2. bringing people who would spend money there

3. it brought the community together

Use a graphic organizer.

Sample answers:

1. The bridge helped people in the community get along.

2. The bridge makes people stop and look more closely.

Prewriting

Answers will vary.

Thinking Beyond Reading

Answers will vary.

Write your sentences.

Use the details in your chart to help you write.

Revise and edit.

Sentences should be complete and use correct spelling and punctuation.

Lesson 5 Sing for Your School
pp. 45–54

Matching Words

1. e

2. b

3. a

4. d

5. c

Sentence Completions

1. accept

2. earned

3. thrilling

4. traditional

5. concert

Word Building

Circle -er or -ier in each word.

2. quicker

3. sharper

4. happier

5. older

Writing Activity

concert

audience

traditional

generation

thrilling

Check your comprehension.

Sample answers:

1. Fisk accepted all men and women.

2. the Fisk Jubilee Singers

3. over $50,000

4. Jubilee Hall

Identify main idea and details.

Sample answers:

1. Underline *Also in that year, the singers went to Europe for the first time.*

2. Circle *They sang for many important and famous people.*

3. give more details about their European concerts

Use a graphic organizer.

Sample answers:

2. Their first concerts were in small towns.

3. At first they weren't successful.

Prewriting

Answers will vary.

Thinking Beyond Reading

Answers will vary.

Write your sentences.

Use the details in your diagram to help you write.

Revise and edit.

Sentences should be complete and use correct spelling and punctuation.

Lesson 6 The Rights of Citizens
pp. 55–64

Matching Words

1. e

2. c

3. b

4. a

5. d

Sentence Completions

1. identification

2. application

3. permisssion

4. ceremony

5. photograph

Word Building

1. rocks

2. foxes

3. families

4. words

5. sandals

6. patches

7. babies

8. crosses

Writing Activity

application

background

fingerprints

process

ceremony

Check your comprehension.

Sample answers:

1. an identification card that says you are allowed to live and work in the United States

2. U.S. government and U.S. history

3. because they can leave the country for more than two years and come back easily

4. The United States declared its independence from England.

Compare and Contrast

Sample answers:

1. cannot vote

2. can travel anywhere, at any time, with their U.S. passports

Use a graphic organizer.

Sample answers:

2. can bring more family members into the country

3. don't have to speak or read English

Prewriting

Answers will vary.

Thinking Beyond Reading
Answers will vary.

Write your sentences.
Use the details in your chart to help you write.

Revise and edit.
Sentences should be complete and use correct spelling and punctuation.

Lesson 7 Learning to Swim
pp. 65–74

Matching Words
1. b
2. d
3. e
4. c
5. a

Sentence Completions
1. nervous
2. glide
3. aisle
4. paused
5. conquer

Word Building
Circle *care, complete, employ, read*
2. happy
3. write
3. use
4. convenient

Writing Activity
suggested

nervous

instructor

glide

conquer

Check your comprehension.
1. Erica
2. goggles
3. a father and son
4. He decides to go back to the swimming class.

Predict outcomes.
1. his swimming class
2. at the edge of the pool
3. sit on the edge of the pool with the rest of the class

Use a graphic organizer.
Sample answers:
2. He'll have fun learning to swim.
3. He'll get scared and leave the class.
4. He'll go back to the class.

Prewriting
Answers will vary.

Thinking Beyond Reading
Answers will vary.

Write your sentences.
Use the details in your chart to help you write.

Revise and edit.
Sentences should be complete and use correct spelling and punctuation.

Lesson 8 Transportation Troubles
pp. 75–84

Matching Words
1. c
2. d
3. b
4. a
5. e

Sentence Completions
1. site
2. transportation
3. interrupted
4. afford
5. exhausted

Word Building
Draw a line in each word: air/plane, lawn/mower, high/chair, cook/book
1. under the ground
2. under the water
3. a shirt worn under another shirt
4. drawing a line under something

Writing Activity

transportation

unfortunately

challenge

afford

exhausted

Check your comprehension.

1. his bus was late

2. his bicycle

3. across the street from his job site

4. because he rode his bicycle

Make inferences.

Sample answers:

1. he thinks his co-workers will make fun of him

2. he doesn't want people to see that he rode a bike to work

3. he feels embarrassed about doing it

Use a graphic organizer.

Sample answers:

1. transportation

2. a long time ago

3. bad about making fun of Lou

Prewriting

Answers will vary.

Thinking Beyond Reading

Answers will vary.

Write your sentences.

Use the details in your chart to help you write.

Revise and edit.

Sentences should be complete and use correct spelling and punctuation.

Lesson 9 Food for Thought
pp. 85–94

Matching Words

1. a

2. e

3. c

4. d

5. b

Sentence Completions

1. recipe

2. handwriting

3. batter

4. ingredients

5. satisfied

Word Building

Underline *pre-, dis-, non-, pre-*

prepay

discomfort

nontraditional

interoffice

antifreeze

Writing Activity

recipe

ingredients

batter

aroma

satisfied

Check your comprehension.

1. her grandmother's biscotti

2. a grater

3. Dan and Christopher

4. her aunt Adela

Identify time order.

Underline *The next evening, First, Next, After about ten minutes, Finally*

Use a graphic organizer.

Sample answers:

2. Then she put them in a large bowl.

3. Next she mixed them together.

4. Then she added more ingredients.

5. Finally she put the cookies in the oven.

Prewriting

Answers will vary.

Thinking Beyond Reading

Answers will vary.

Write your sentences.

Use the details in your chart to help you write.

Revise and edit.
Sentences should be complete and use correct spelling and punctuation.

Lesson 10 Trading Clothes, Saving Money pp. 95–104

Matching Words

1. c
2. d
3. a
4. e
5. b

Sentence Completions

1. manages
2. variety
3. admission
4. recycle
5. full-length

Word Building

Circle -ness in each word.

1. brightness
2. Sleepiness
3. soreness
4. loudness

Writing Activity

swap

recycle

fee

variety

opportunity

Check your comprehension.

1. a place where people can trade clothing
2. to cover the cost of renting the space
3. at your house
4. It is taken to a thrift shop.

Synthesize information.
Sample answers:

1. shoes, belts, purses, scarves, hats
2. shoes, accessories, jewelry
3. I can take my _____ to a clothing swap.

Use a graphic organizer.
Sample answers, second column:

2. Clothing swaps have children's clothing.
3. People make money by having clothing swaps.

Sample answers, third column:

2. I can get my kids some clothes at a clothing swap.
3. I can make money by having a clothing swap.

Prewriting
Answers will vary.

Thinking Beyond Reading
Answers will vary.

Write your sentences.
Use the details in your chart to help you write.

Revise and edit.
Sentences should be complete and use correct spelling and punctuation.